EBURY PRESS

KHAK

Neeraj Kumar is one of the most distinguished officers to have served in the Indian Police. He joined the IPS in 1976 and retired as the commissioner of police, Delhi, in 2013.

While on deputation with the Central Bureau of Investigation (CBI), first as deputy inspector general and then as joint director, he investigated several sensational cases and conducted a number of transnational operations involving terrorism, organized crime, economic offences and corruption. He was later appointed as the joint commissioner of police, Special Cell of the Delhi Police—mainly responsible for tackling Pakistan-sponsored terrorism—and the director general of prisons, Delhi.

In an illustrious career spanning thirty-seven years, Kumar held a range of high-profile assignments and ushered in novel initiatives, such as Padho aur Padhao, a literacy and placement scheme for prisoners; Aapka Update, a scheme for providing regular updates to complainants on police action; and Jan Sampark, a platform for members of the public to meet senior police officers and air their grievances.

Kumar represented India at the UN Convention on Transnational Organized Crime in Vienna and later at the drafting session of the UN Manual on Countering Kidnapping and Extortion. The Government of India recognized his good work by awarding him the Police Medal for Meritorious Service in 1993 and the President's Police Medal for Distinguished Service in 1999. Kumar, till recently, headed the Anti-corruption and Security Unit of the Board of Control for Cricket in India (BCCI).

Khaki Files is his second book, whose stories are the subject of a web series under production.

ALSO BY THE SAME AUTHOR

Dial D for Don

ADVANCE PRAISE FOR *KHAKI FILES*

'Neeraj Kumar brings his varied experience as a top cop to give us the inside track to the dark world of crime. Highly readable, *Khaki Files* is a real page-turner'—**Rajdeep Sardesai**

'Mr Neeraj Kumar's gift as a storyteller lies in the fact that he tells it the way it is. Very rarely do we find a narrative that sits on the edge of such believability and impossibility'—**Neeraj Pandey**

'Neeraj Kumar has had an illustrious career as one of India's most admired strategic policing minds. In any job that he has undertaken, he has left his mark because of his integrity, innovation and inspired leadership. His first book, *Dial D for Don*, laid bare the machinations of the Indian mafia's diabolical world and the Indian police's marvellous job at restraining them.

'In this new book, *Khaki Files*, he fascinates the reader with both the repertoire and substance of the manner in which the police, under his leadership, could crack cases ranging from lottery fraud to terrorism. *Khaki Files* is not just a compendium of great tales told with riveting accuracy but is also a book that any chronicler of India's criminality would benefit from reading. The evocative power of the chosen stories and the manner in which he weaves the tales with deftness and suspense make for brilliant scholarship and reading'—**Suhel Seth**

S. HUSSAIN ZAIDI PRESENTS

KHAKI

FILES

Inside
Stories of
Police
Investigations

NEERAJ KUMAR

**BLUE
SALT**

EBURY
PRESS

An imprint of Penguin Random House

EBURY PRESS

USA | Canada | UK | Ireland | Australia
New Zealand | India | South Africa | China

Ebury Press is part of the Penguin Random House group of companies
whose addresses can be found at global.penguinrandomhouse.com

Published by Penguin Random House India Pvt. Ltd
7th Floor, Infinity Tower C, DLF Cyber City,
Gurgaon 122 002, Haryana, India

Penguin
Random House
India

First published in Ebury Press and Blue Salt by Penguin Random House India 2019

ISBN 9780143428008

Typeset in Adobe Garamond Pro by Manipal Digital Systems, Manipal
Printed at Replika Press Pvt. Ltd, India

www.penguin.co.in

MIX
Paper from
responsible sources
FSC® C016779

To my colleagues, who have known and shared my passion for policing; to my two granddaughters, Aishwarya and Dhvani, who have taught me the true meaning of joy; and to my dear wife, Mala, who has lived with me every moment of agony and ecstasy that life in the police brought me

Contents

Contents

Foreword

When the author sounded me out to write the foreword to his second book, *Khaki Files*, I agreed without hesitation, though the word that came to my mind was déjà vu. But I was so impressed with his earlier work, *Dial D for Don*, that I welcomed his proposal most willingly. And, what a delightful experience it has been. *Khaki Files* is written so stylishly. What he has now produced is a thrilling work, not of fiction but real-life experiences that called for acutely skillful leadership, which he has displayed all along.

More than anything else, what fascinated me were the elements of autobiography (at times somewhat poignant), especially when it comes to his unpleasant personal experiences with some of his seniors and colleagues. Neeraj has shown grace and large-heartedness in not naming them. He has also avoided naming his political masters who meant him harm.

While each chapter is a fascinating experience, the first one on the lottery scam, 'A Matter of Chance', made a huge impression. Apart from an occasional purchase of lottery tickets—what is called lotto in New York—I had no experience of lotteries. So Neeraj's narration was a shocking eye-opener. It shows that lotteries were never a matter of chance, but an organized racket by habitual cheats to dupe the common man. Those who repeatedly keep on trying their luck in lotteries are unaware that they are putting themselves at the receiving end of a game of fraud. In this story, a common man, Pritam Kumar Razak, in December 1991, wins Rs 51 lakh in a lottery. Naturally, he is overjoyed not knowing that what awaits him is not Rs 51 lakh, but an unending period of tension, disappointment and denial of what are his legitimate dues, all on account of a fraud perpetrated on him by a network of crooks. Had the author and his team not unearthed the scam run by these crooks, perhaps the racket of lotteries would have continued to hoodwink people for a long time. To the immense credit of Neeraj and his team of Delhi Police, lotteries by private persons and bodies are thereafter banned by an order of the Supreme Court, sparing the people of perpetual fraud.

Another most fascinating account is the 'Da Lakhvi Code' (like *Da Vinci Code* by Dan Brown). It is about a terror attack plot by the ISI, to organize a well-orchestrated and diabolical bomb blast on the hallowed portal of India Gate in Delhi on 25 February 2003, not too long after the attack on India's Parliament in 2001. The terrorists expected to kill maybe several hundred Indians gathered to relax and enjoy the amazingly mild weather of Delhi at that time of the year, hoping to replicate the horrendous serial Bombay blasts of 1993. To the good luck of Pakistan, the plot failed! Had it succeeded, they would have had hell to pay at the hands of India.

The decision-makers of the ISI should by now realize that trans-border terror attacks would not help them grab Kashmir or weaken or destroy India in any way. India is too big a country with huge resources at its command and has the wherewithal to withstand such dastardly strikes and retaliate in ample measure. In any case, neither side can afford to let their longstanding dispute blow up into a nuclear conflagration.

Another chapter 'Devil's Advocate' brings to the fore the noble side of the author's personality. During the post–Mandal Commission riots in 1990, the media showed the police lifting the bullet-ridden body of an agitator at INA Market in New Delhi in a crude, ungainly way. The visuals caused public uproar and led to a lot of adverse criticism. A public interest litigation was filed in the Delhi High Court against the police of the district of which Neeraj was the DCP, and where the riots took place.

Two decades later, while he was the director general of prisons, Delhi, he came across a convict named Manjeet Singh, serving life sentence for killing Bawa Gurcharan Singh, an eminent advocate of Delhi. In fact, it was Bawa who had come to the rescue of the author and his officers in Delhi Police in defending them successfully in the public interest litigation filed in the Delhi High Court. This was after various lawyers who had been sounded out did not want to come to the rescue of the Delhi Police, given the political implications and the general mood of the public at large. The convict Manjeet Singh was sentenced to life imprisonment for the murder of the advocate. He served his term in Delhi's Tihar Jail for a full 'nineteen years six months and ten days'.

Eventually, Neeraj, overcoming his personal grouse with Manjeet Singh who had murdered his saviour, took up his case in a meeting of the Sentence Review Board that met under the chief minister of Delhi. In the face of strident objections from other members of the Board, he was successful in saving Manjeet Singh from further incarceration. As the author says, '[H]elping Manjeet Singh walk free gave (him) a different kind of high that is too difficult to describe.'

The author's account of his Goa stint reminded me of my own tenure as chief of police of Pondicherry (now Puducherry), on the eastern coast of India. But what Neeraj went through was a macrocosmic experience compared to my rather microcosmic exposure to the vagaries of political interference in police work. Pondicherry was an unglamorous, sleepy town, unlike the rocking and scintillating Goa. There were no rave parties and fewer visitors to the town, except maybe the spiritually inclined, who would visit the Aurobindo Ashram and the nearby township of Auroville.

Another intriguing account from Neeraj's book is 'Moon-gazer'. Till the British were in occupation of India, we had what the British called 'criminal tribes', spread almost all over the country. Crimes of robbery, accompanied by violence and murder, were their acknowledged profession. As the author says, they 'would break into homes, bludgeon the residents to death in their sleep without any provocation and then ransack their homes, looking for jewellery, cash, wristwatches and other small items of value. If spotted by the police, they would throw stones at them, sometimes injuring them severely'. They gave the police a lot of anxious time till Neeraj and his team ran them into the ground.

All in all, *Khaki Files* is a most readable collection of true crime stories that gives an insight into the extraordinary challenges that our police face, almost on a day-to-day basis. It equally shows how they acquit themselves creditably every time the situation demands of them high degree of professionalism and skill. The author brings both sides of this conundrum to us in a compelling narrative.

Raja Vijay Karan
Former commissioner of police, Delhi,
and former director of the CBI

Preface

I had written my first book *Dial D for Don* with considerable trepidation and diffidence. Uncertain whether my writing skills were adequate to meet the exacting standards of a published work, I soldiered on, nonetheless, as I was confident that my stories were worthy of being told and heard. The book, an anthology of eleven accounts of Central Bureau of Investigation (CBI) operations conducted during the nine years I spent in the central investigative agency, was a decent success. Besides figuring on several bestseller lists for weeks, the book also elicited considerable interest from producers of web series, and film-makers were keen on buying the rights of the book. The overwhelming but humbling approbation makes both my publishers and me believe that there exists a considerable readership of true crime stories written in first-person singular by a senior police officer.

The celebrated Mumbai-based crime writer S. Hussain Zaidi, who had initiated me into writing the first book, encouraged me to write again using the same template. Despite my initial reluctance, I decided, egged on by Milee

Ashwarya of Penguin Random House and Zaidi sahib, to take another plunge.

I always thought writing the second book would be much easier than the first one. However, the experience of the first book had neither given me the habit nor the discipline of writing regularly. To make matters worse, my preoccupation with the Board of Control for Cricket in India (BCCI), as the head of its anti-corruption and security unit, denied me the right frame of mind necessary to start writing again. Fortuitously, by an unexpected turn of events, I quit my job with the cricket body on 31 May 2018. The following day I was on my desk and my writing resumed.

Khaki Files is a collection of nine stories based on my experiences in different assignments—ranging from deputy commissioner of police (DCP) of south district in Delhi to director general of police (DGP) of Goa, and finally as commissioner of police (CP) of Delhi. They cover over three decades of my career in the police. In most of these recollections, I was leading the investigations, and, in a couple of them—'Sovereignty under Siege' and 'Stories of Their Assassins'—I was a close witness to the probes. Two other stories—'Devil's Advocate' and 'Goan Rhapsody'—do not strictly relate to investigations but are, I feel, interesting and readable nuggets from my memory bank. I sincerely hope the readers like these stories as much as they appreciated those in *Dial D for Don*.

I can't help but question myself whether writing about cases I have been associated with serves any meaningful purpose, besides entertaining readers with true stories of crime and criminals. It is comforting to imagine that, willly-nilly,

I have documented, for the benefit of posterity, accounts of police work that would otherwise be never known. For instance, the story 'Sovereignty under Siege' brings into the public domain an account of the investigation into the Parliament House terror attack case . Similarly, 'Da Lakhvi Code' is a hitherto unknown tale of a cyber investigation that prevented a terror attack at India Gate. Further, 'Moon-gazer' recounts how serial killings and robberies by members of an erstwhile criminal tribe were worked out in the early 1990s, and how the capital was saved from their depredations ever since.

Police officers behind such probes remain unknown and unsung. Even in a case like the Parliament House terror attack, the officers who solved the case in less than seventy-two hours hardly received any recognition. Had a similar case been solved in another country, say the US, I am sure the police team concerned would have received an invite to the White House for tea with the American president, besides being felicitated in other ways. Cover stories on them would have appeared in prestigious magazines like *Time* and *Newsweek*. But no such thing ever happens in our country. We are adept at police-bashing, but always fail to acknowledge their good work. Quite unconsciously, by telling these stories, I strive to bring their good work to the fore, for whatever it is worth.

Whether we like it or not, each one of us leaves behind a legacy, if not for the big wide world, at least for our near and dear ones. It can be a house, some money or, if nothing else, some stories or memories. With *Dial D for Don* and *Khaki Files*, the twenty police stories that I have narrated, I sincerely hope, would become a part of my modest legacy.

1

A Matter of Chance

Pritam Kumar Razak, a petty worker with the locomotive workshop in Jamalpur, Bihar, was a happy man, content with what he had in life—a secure job, a caring wife and two lovely children. He had no bad habits except, perhaps, one: he spent a lot of money on buying lottery tickets, hoping someday Lady Luck would smile on him and make him rich overnight.

Sure enough, the fateful day dawned on 6 December 1991. Ticket number SA-763447, which he had bought for the bumper draw of the All India Deaf and Dumb Society Lotteries, run under the aegis of the Andhra Pradesh (AP) government, was declared the winner of the first prize of Rs 51 lakh. Now, Rs 51 lakh at that time—or for that matter even now—was a lot of money. Pritam's jubilation knew no bounds and he celebrated by distributing sweets amongst his friends and neighbours, who were more envious than happy for him. Both his wife and he began to plan how they would invest the money to secure their children's future, after setting aside some money for themselves. They would perhaps take that elusive trip to Goa, a place they had heard so much about and dreamt of visiting some day. Little did they realize that one should never count one's chickens before they hatch.

An excited Pritam went to meet the manager of the local branch of the State Bank of India, who processed his claim—as was the procedure prescribed to claim winnings in the said lottery—and sent the winning ticket along with other necessary documents to the society's office in New Delhi. Interestingly, the society responded by sending two different acknowledgements of receipt: one to the bank and the other to Pritam. The communication he received said that the society had received all necessary documents except the winning ticket, whereas the bank was informed that all documents had been duly received.

A disturbed Pritam Kumar entered into a protracted correspondence with the society stating that his bank had sent them the winning ticket, but his protests were to no avail. After running from pillar to post, he was advised to approach the Crime Branch of the Delhi Police where Assistant Commissioner of Police (ACP) S.M. Bhaskar heard his complaint and immediately sensed foul play. He deputed Sub-inspector (SI) O.P. Sagar to look into the matter.

A case of cheating, criminal conspiracy and theft was registered on the basis of Pritam's complaint and an investigation was launched. The SI interrogated the employees concerned of the All India Deaf and Dumb Society in Delhi, who denied having received the winning ticket. It came to light that they had outsourced the running of the lottery to M/s Popular Ventures & Capitals Private Limited, who in turn had appointed M/s Bharat Lottery as their sole selling agent.

SI Sagar, the investigating officer (IO), was surprised when Praveen Kumar Jolly of Bharat Lottery said that the winning ticket had never been printed. Thus, the fraud perpetrated by Jolly was evident. The IO reported his findings to ACP Bhaskar, who instructed him to get to the bottom of the case by visiting Hyderabad and contacting the lottery department officials of the AP government since the Deaf and Dumb Society claimed to have the department's approval.

When the SI inquired of the officials whether they had authorized the society to conduct the lottery, he was in for another shock. The society had been given permission to run a lottery only for its own members and not for the general public. Thus, the lottery that was being run by the society was unlawful.

As the probe went deeper, layer after layer of fraudulent activities began to emerge. The society had never approached the AP government for permission to hold a bumper draw. It conducted the bumper draw without the government's approval and had also printed on the tickets that it was a government-approved draw of lots. No government official was present when the draw was carried out. Therefore, the society had given the public the false impression that it was organizing a lottery that had the approval of the AP government, when in reality it was running a private, unauthorized and fraudulent lottery.

There was yet another act of chicanery involved. The scheme ostensibly envisaged a total of twenty-four lakh tickets, and this information was printed on the back of the tickets. In reality, the organizers printed only 2,40,000 tickets. However, when the draw for the winning tickets was done, the numbers of all twenty-four lakh tickets were included whereas only 2,40,000 tickets had been sold. This meant that chances of the balance 21,60,000 unsold/ unprinted tickets remained with the organizers, which was 90 per cent! Further, if any one of the printed tickets were to win a prize, it would only be of Rs 50 each, as had been decided beforehand by the organizers.

Thus, assuming that all printed tickets were sold, they would yield Rs 1,20,00,000, whereas only Rs 12,000 was to be paid by way of prizes. In this manner, a single draw yielded a profit of Rs 1,19,80,000 to the organizers, which was shared amongst the selling agents, the organizing company and the society. The figures were mind-boggling, and with hundreds of lotteries under operation with multiple daily draws in quite a few of them, the Crime Branch was sitting on the tip of an enormous iceberg. There was a lottery scam running across the country, cheating millions of people of their hard-earned money, and the Crime Branch had to do everything it could to stem the rot.

* * *

I had completed an eventful three-year stint as the deputy commissioner of police (DCP), south district, in August 1992 and was desperate for a change of assignment. District jobs can get stressful and tedious after a while, and I was a tad weary and longing for a change, having carried the yoke for over three years. I requested the then commissioner of police (CP), M.B. Kaushal, to transfer me out, and he very kindly posted me as DCP, Crime Branch of the Delhi Police, an assignment after my heart. To my good fortune, the multi-crore lottery scam came my way within just over a month of my joining, and it turned out to be one of the most satisfying investigations of my career.

As the word spread about the Pritam Kumar Razak lottery fraud case, many more complainants who had been cheated similarly began to approach the Crime Branch. During the investigation of each case, newer and more bizarre ways employed by the lottery operators to cheat people began to emerge. One such case was that of Jasminder Singh, a resident of Bhagat Singh Market in New Delhi, who had won a prize in a daily draw of the Jeevan Rekha lottery, ostensibly run under the aegis of the Government of Manipur.

When Jasminder approached the lottery owners with his winning ticket, he was informed that there had been a mistake in the printing of the results in the newspapers. It was claimed that the results of Jeevan Rekha and Vijay Rekha had been erroneously interchanged, and it was an innocent printing error. Usually, when a purchaser of lottery tickets reads in the papers that his ticket number has not figured in the list of prizes, he destroys the tickets. Now, with this interchanging of the results many genuine prizewinners would have thrown their tickets away. Jasminder Singh, however, went to the police station in Karol Bagh to register a complaint that he had been cheated of Rs 1 lakh. The local police directed him to approach the Crime Branch as we had already investigated a case of lottery fraud.

When the case came to us, we learnt that M/s Guru Nanak Agency, Karol Bagh, run by one S.K. Sethi, was the sole selling agent for Manipur State Lotteries. They paid Rs 18,000 as fixed royalty on each of the daily draws of Jeevan Rekha, Bhagya Rekha, Vijay Rekha and Bhagya Rekha Super—four lotteries run by them for the Manipur government. Thus, the organizers paid a fixed royalty of Rs 2,10,00,000 per annum to the Manipur government.

S.K. Sethi defrauded unsuspecting lottery ticket buyers by interchanging the results of Jeevan Rekha and Vijay Rekha lotteries in the newspapers. Generally, members of the public go by the results published in the newspapers. By interchanging the results of the two lotteries, Sethi made a wrongful gain of Rs 2.5 crore in one single draw.

Readers can extrapolate the amount of money Sethi would have made by adopting this modus operandi when the draw of lots took place every day. Not even in one case did Sethi issue a corrigendum. After registering a case based on the complaint made by Jasminder Singh and conducting a detailed investigation, we arrested S.K. Sethi on 11 November 1992 and charge-sheeted him for cheating and criminal breach of trust.

Yet another complainant, Jagdish Lal of Faridabad, bought Hast Rekha lottery ticket number 3851501, which was declared the first prize winner in the draw of lots in June 1993. The prize amount was Rs 1 lakh. Much like Pritam Kumar Razak of Jamalpur, he sent his claim through a nationalized bank, but the organizing agent did not pay him a single penny on the ground that the ticket in question was never printed. When Jagdish Lal persisted with his questioning of the organizing agent, he was threatened with criminal action for forgery.

S.K. Sethi was once again the organizing agent. We recovered Jagdish Lal's prize-winning ticket from Sethi's office. Additional charges were pressed against Sethi, who had already been arrested by the Crime Branch in the earlier case.

Complaints of lottery frauds committed by resorting to a wide variety of modus operandi continued to pour in. Ved Prakash Saxena of Bareilly complained that he was denied payment of the first prize of the Bharat Raffle Deluxe Lottery on his winning ticket number 321138, which amounted to Rs 2 lakh. M/s Guru Nanak Lotteries of Karol Bagh had organized the draw in May 1993. Here again, the organizing agent questioned the genuineness of the ticket Saxena produced and shooed away the claimant by threatening him with criminal action for forgery. When the matter reached the Crime Branch, the office of Guru Nanak Lotteries was searched and the winning ticket recovered. V.S. Sethi, a brother of S.K. Sethi, was arrested in this case.

Another lottery agency, M/s APS Agencies, was investigated on the basis of a complaint received at the police station on Deshbandhu Gupta Road, New Delhi. In this case, the company was not only cheating ticket buyers of their rightful prize money but was also forging its accounts, showing false transactions in its books and evading taxes amounting to crores of rupees.

The said agency was the sole organizer of Matka Sone Ka (MSK) and Matka Motiyon Ka (MMK)—two daily lotteries authorized by the Punjab government. The company was also authorized to supply paper for the printing of tickets while M/s Druck Grafen India Private Limited was contracted for printing the tickets.

The book of accounts revealed that M/s Druck Grafen procured the paper from APS Agencies and printed tickets at the rate of Rs 1500 per lakh. Nearly Rs 23 lakh was paid as expenditure on paper to APS Agencies and Rs 30 lakh was shown as printing charges. Further scrutiny of records revealed that one M/s Krishna Paper Mart supplied the paper to APS Agencies. However, investigations revealed that M/s Krishna Paper Mart was a non-existent firm and its registered office was the residence of a private citizen. The sales tax office also confirmed that no such firm had been allotted the sales tax number that the books of Druck Grafen reflected as belonging to their 'paper supplier'. Further, mandatory government papers meant for transportation of stationery from Delhi to Patiala did not carry any central sales tax or local sales tax numbers. It was clear that the bogus firm had not supplied any stationery, and all the bills in the books of Druck Grafen concerning M/s Krishna Paper Mart were fraudulent.

APS Agencies' books revealed that Rs 23 lakh had been paid to M/s Krishna Paper Mart for the supply of paper and Rs 30 lakh to Druck Grafen for the printing of lottery tickets. Since Krishna Paper Mart was a fictitious entity, the paper could not have been procured from them. Investigations also revealed how this money had been swindled by dubious bank dealings carried out by APS Agencies and Druck Grafen. Needless to say, no taxes had been paid to the exchequer for these dealings.

To top it all, APS Agencies denied its lottery winners access to prize money by one trick or the other. The winning buyer had to claim his or her money within forty-five days of the announcement of the prize and had to make the claim through the office of the Punjab State Lotteries. The office, after ascertaining the genuineness of the tickets, was supposed to send the claim to APS Agencies, which would make the money available to the lottery office that would then disburse the money to the winner. The lottery department of the Punjab government furnished a list of 246 draws of Matka Sone Ka and 102 draws of Matka Motiyon Ka. It was astonishing to find that only thirty-one claims for prize money out of 246 draws of MSK and fifteen claims out of 102 draws of MMK were made. A total of only Rs 5 lakh stood disbursed out of the Rs 6.91 crore that was kept reserved for prizes. The balance amount of Rs 6.86 crore had been swindled. It was also clear that officials of the Punjab lottery department had not supervised the conduct of lotteries closely, and were, perhaps, part of the scam.

It was no surprise, therefore, that officials of the lottery departments of various states, including Punjab, were camping in Delhi during our investigation, trying their best to twist our arms. Since our superiors supported us and we stood our ground, we had little difficulty in withstanding the pressure tactics. Interestingly, many media houses came forward in support of the lottery operators as their advertising revenues were being negatively affected by our investigation.

The above-mentioned facts relate to only a handful of cases investigated by the Crime Branch. It would not be incorrect to say that similar frauds existed in all 137 lotteries being run in Delhi, out of which quite a few had daily draws. We estimated that countrywide, around Rs 55,000 crore of people's money had been swindled in the lottery scam. We arrived at this figure by working backwards after obtaining the aggregate of royalties that the state governments had received from lottery operators. No government agency, no civil society organization, or, for that matter, no section of the media had taken notice of this scam of humongous proportions. The reasons were simple and straightforward. The lottery departments of various state governments, whose responsibility it was to regulate such lotteries, were themselves party to the scam and had a vested interest in perpetuating the malpractices. The victims were poor, powerless and faceless citizens of the country, who could be turned away or silenced easily by any agency they approached with their grievances. The lottery operators, government officials and unscrupulous politicians made tons of money at the cost of the poorest of the poor. It is no surprise that when their unbridled run at making easy money came to an abrupt end—as will be described later—most of the lottery operators shut shop and invested their ill-gotten money in real estate and other capital-intensive enterprises.

* * *

When someone buys a lottery ticket, they do so under the impression that a reasonably fair chance to win a prize exists. However, investigations into the above cases revealed that the odds were heavily against the ticket buyers as the sellers of this chance manipulated the conduct of lotteries in such a way that they cornered the odds and the bulk of the proceeds of the lottery went into their own pockets. The buyers received prizes only on the rarest of rare occasions. To understand the malpractices in this trade, I decided to probe the matter in great depth with my team and studied every modus operandi adopted by lottery operators and catalogued them. But before I go into the outcome of this investigation, let us understand the legal aspect of the situation.

In its legal and popular sense, 'lottery' means distribution of prizes by lots or chance. It is the purchase of this chance that is the essence of a lottery. The distinction between lottery and gambling is subtle as both are games of chance. But gambling is a game played by and in the presence of all participants while in the case of a lottery, the presence of participants is both unnecessary and superfluous. In gambling, there may be a display of some skill, as in rolling a dice or the like. In a lottery, the participants merely buy chance, the happening of which is beyond their control. The mischief of gambling affects only the actual players whereas in a lottery it is widespread. The US Supreme Court observed:

> Experience has shown that the common forms of gambling are comparatively innocuous when placed in contrast with the widespread pestilence of lotteries. The former are confined to a few persons and places, but the latter infests the whole community. It enters every class, it preys upon the hard earnings of the poor, and plunders the ignorant and the simple.[*]

The law reprobates gambling as well as the lottery because both promote the circulation of money that is the fruit of

---

[*] Supreme Court of America in *Phaten vs. Commonwealth of Virginia*, (1850) 49 US 163: 12 Law Ed. 1030 at p. 1033 (z).

labour by chance, a practice that is both unjust and unequal. Furthermore, gambling and lottery encourage the squandering of hard-earned money, which leads to incalculable misery. They are, moreover, in opposition to honest labour and thrift, upon which the happiness of society depends. An English court called 'keepers of lotteries as a class of rogues and vagabonds', and they are, in fact, so. Lotteries are mostly intended to inveigle people into purchasing worthless things or parting with their money with no return, to the advantage of the lottery keeper. As such, a lottery is a fraudulent public practice because it leads people to pay for a game in which there is no subtlety—namely, that the lottery keeper keeps the biggest prize.

The subject of lottery figures in the Union list of the Constitution of India in Entry No. 40 of the Seventh Schedule. However, curiously, the Centre had not legislated on the subject, thereby leaving the ground clear for a free-for-all situation. This was the beginning of all the troubles in the Indian context. If the Central government had spelt out the dos and don'ts for the lottery trade and had enabled law enforcement agencies to come down heavily on violations, the large-scale loot of people would have stopped. In the absence of any legislation, some state governments, such as Andhra Pradesh and Karnataka, enacted their own laws. For instance, Section 3 of the Andhra Pradesh Lotteries Act of 1968 declares that all lotteries are unlawful. However, under Section 24, the Act gives some exemptions to a lottery whose net proceeds are to be used for charitable or educational purposes. Under the garb of this provision, several lotteries run by unscrupulous individuals got authorizations from the

AP government and ran private lotteries. Some such lotteries that came to adverse notice were:

1. All India Deaf and Dumb Society
2. Visakhapatnam District Cricket Association
3. Urban and Rural Development Scheme
4. Share Medical Care

Section 294 A of the Indian Penal Code provides that running of any lottery that is not a state lottery or a lottery authorized by the state government is an offence. However, Section 294 A is non-cognizable and bailable, which means that the police cannot take action without a court's permission and the accused, if arrested, has to be released on bail immediately.

By several judicial pronouncements and orders of the government, both state and Central, only a lottery that is initiated and managed by the state government is permissible. The rest come under the category of private lotteries, which are banned.

However, the trick of the trade was to somehow get an authorization from the lottery department of a state government for running a lottery, for which a small amount of royalty was paid to state authorities. Regrettably, the lottery departments, having given such authorization, ceded control to the private lottery operators. Nobody knew when and where the draws were held; nobody knew who attended the draws and whether any representative of the government was present. Thus, the lottery operators could do what they wanted.

The second and most reprehensible act of chicanery was to print far fewer tickets than were declared in the scheme.

For instance, if the scheme envisaged twenty lakh tickets, only two lakh tickets were printed. Further, not all two lakh tickets printed were sold. However, when the draws took place, not only were all twenty lakh ticket numbers approved by the lottery department concerned included, but also included were the unsold ticket numbers, reducing the chance of a valid ticket buyer winning a prize by more than 90 per cent. All chances accruing out of unprinted and unsold tickets stayed with the lottery operator. Thus, over 90 per cent of the time, the prize-winning tickets were those that were with the operator himself.

If even against these adverse odds a valid ticket buyer won a prize, the lottery operator would turn away such a ticket holder, claiming that the ticket was never printed and the claimant was producing a forged ticket. The poor man was threatened with legal action for forgery. At the beginning of this story we saw how lottery organizers shooed away Pritam Kumar Razak of Jamalpur and Jasminder Singh of New Delhi, denying them their legitimate prize money and holding on to every penny of the cash paid by ticket buyers from across the country.

Emboldened by the lack of oversight by government officials, the lottery operators adopted a more depraved method: they printed and sold only forged tickets. When the draws were conducted, the numbers used were of another series, which had been approved by the government lottery department. So the numbers of the tickets sold were not used in the draw at all. That meant the buyers had zero chance of winning and all the proceeds of the ticket sales went directly into the pockets of the operators.

An even more diabolical way of cheating lottery ticket buyers was to interchange the results of two lotteries, thereby denying prizes to legitimate prizewinners. This method of cheating came to light, as narrated earlier in this chapter, when the results of Jeevan Rekha and Vijay Rekha were deliberately interchanged. Here again, the organizers conveniently pocketed all sale proceeds.

By adopting these tactics, the lottery operators denied disbursement of prizes, especially prizes of higher denominations, to any genuine ticket holder.

* * *

On 31 May 1993, four lottery operators from Delhi were returning from Kohima in a private taxi when the insurgent group, People's Liberation Army (PLA) of Manipur, gunned them down. The PLA had warned the Manipur government of direct action against lottery operators if the government failed to ban them. The PLA felt, and perhaps rightly so, that innocent Manipuri people had been cheated by non-Manipuri private lottery organizers for several years. Their contention was that while lakhs of people from Manipur had bought lottery tickets, not a single Manipuri had ever received a prize because of fraud in the conduct of lotteries. The PLA had urged the Manipur government to stop lottery trade in their state. However, when after several warnings the state government did not take any action, they resorted to this killing.

Criminal incidents related to the lottery trade occurred in different parts of the country from time to time. In some cases, lottery operators resorted to killing fellow operators out of professional rivalry and in turf wars. In others, lottery ticket buyers, having lost their hard-earned money, committed suicide.

Since a lot of data emerged during our investigations, I decided to collate them in the form of a monograph that bore the same title as the present chapter. Besides a detailed note on the various modus operandi adopted by the lottery operators, it had copies of all relevant government orders, a list of lottery operators, the number of draws held by them, the prizes disbursed, etc. The monograph was in high demand by various state police forces, lottery department officials and police stations in Delhi. Besides circulating it to these recipients, I sent a copy of the monograph to the Ministry of Home Affairs (MHA), which dealt with the subject in the Government of India.

Following the action taken by the Delhi Police, several lottery vendors wound up their operations and closed shop. In some states such as Bihar, Haryana and Madhya Pradesh, the state governments banned lotteries. Lottery operators across India came together and decided to approach the Supreme Court regarding the action being taken by the state and the Central governments as well as the police cases against them. The best lawyers of the country represented them. During the proceedings, after hearing the arguments of both sides, the court asked the government counsel if any systematic study had been conducted by the government into the frauds committed by lottery operators. In the absence of any other report, MHA submitted the monograph prepared by us. Copies were supplied to the advocates of the lottery operators as well. After protracted hearings, the court adjourned for final orders to a date a fortnight later, when it would decide the fate of lottery operators in India.

We waited with bated breath for the hearing, eager to know what the court had to say about our findings on this mammoth fraud, which had illegally lined the pockets of a few unscrupulous lottery vendors, devastated the lives of thousands of innocent lottery ticket buyers and defrauded the government of billions of rupees by tax evasion and tax fraud. We were a humble team of a few police officers armed only with a monograph on our meticulous investigations and represented by a senior government counsel. The lottery vendors were a wealthy force, had the media on their side due to the enormous advertising revenue made through such operators, the best lawyers of the land, and the support of a few unscrupulous politicians and lottery department officials. I hoped the Supreme Court would deem our findings meritorious and substantial and stop lottery vendors from looting millions of innocent people of their hard-earned money in the future.

The date of the hearing finally arrived. The bench, in the opening lines of their order, quoted from *A Matter of Chance*. The court took note of the cases we had investigated and appreciated the pioneering work we had done, much like a sustained campaign. In a far-reaching order, the court put a blanket ban on all private lotteries and declared only those that were run wholly by the government to be legal.

As the officer who had studied and investigated the lottery frauds in the country for months, the order was gratifying.

What was even more humbling was the fact that the court had relied heavily on the monograph I had prepared with the help of my ACP, S.M. Bhaskar.

Millions of innocent people, who would have otherwise been the victims of such frauds in subsequent years, had been saved. That was reward enough for us; that was the recognition to be cherished forever.

2

The Da Lakhvi Code

India Gate is a war memorial located astride Rajpath, on the eastern edge of the 'ceremonial axis' of New Delhi, formerly called Kingsway. On this edifice are inscribed the names of more than 70,000 soldiers of the British Indian Army who died in the First World War and the Third Anglo-Afghan War during the period 1914–21.

Though a war memorial, India Gate evokes the architectural style of triumphal arches such as the Arch of Constantine in Rome and the Arc de Triomphe in Paris. It was designed by Sir Edwin Lutyens—arguably one of the greatest English architects—as part of India's new imperial capital, which later became the seat of the Government of India after the country gained independence in 1947.

Built between 1921 and 1931, the memorial stands 42 metres high and is made of Bharatpur stone. Surrounding the imposing structure is a large expanse of lush green lawns, which is a popular picnic spot. One can see throngs of people moving about the memorial and on the lawns all day, and particularly in the evenings, when it is dramatically floodlit with the fountains nearby, creating a lovely display. The story that follows recounts a police operation to save the thousands of visitors to India Gate area from what could have been a disastrous terror attack. This is the first time that this hitherto well-kept secret is being brought into the public domain.

* * *

In the autumn of 2002, with terror raging in the Kashmir Valley and other parts of India, ACP Pramod Kushwaha of the Special Cell of Delhi Police visited Srinagar. He was investigating a terror case in Delhi, and as was his wont, besides his investigative work, his mission was also to collect intelligence on terrorists operating in the country. He met with several local officers serving in the Valley in his quest for information, one of whom was a deputy commandant of the Border Security Force (BSF). The BSF officer had been involved in several armed altercations with Pakistan-sponsored terrorists trying to cross the international border. He was impressed with Pramod's professional enthusiasm and his wide knowledge of crime and criminals. He showed Pramod a diary recovered from one of the slain terrorists, killed in an encounter with a BSF team under his command. Amongst the many diary entries that he saw, the ACP took a mental note of an email address scribbled innocuously on the last page.

The Special Cell of the Delhi Police was founded in 1986 in the wake of rising terrorism in the country. Delhi, being the national capital and seat of government, was always in the cross hairs of terror groups. Any attack here was bound to attract worldwide attention and huge international publicity. Fighting terrorism was the raison d'être of the cell, which had evolved over the years into an elite unit of the Delhi Police with many commendable successes to its credit. It had also proved to be a scourge for interstate organized criminal gangs. It had cracked several sensational cases such as the terror attack on the Indian Parliament House on 13 December 2001 that left fourteen dead (including five terrorists). This was believed to be a joint operation of two terror outfits based in Pakistan, namely, Jaish-e-Mohammed (JeM) and Lashkar-e-Taiba (LeT). It also handled the Red Fort terror attack case of 22 December 2000, in which two army men and one civilian were killed; busted many cells of the Hizbul Mujahideen (HM), Indian Mujahideen (IM), LeT, JeM and Babbar Khalsa; arrested numerous interstate gangsters such as Fazl-ur-Rehman, Munna Bajrangi, Brajesh Singh, Sher Singh (accused in the Phoolan Devi murder case) and O.P. Singh, and so on. Undeniably, it had proven to be the nemesis of terror groups and organized criminal gangs that were planning to make Delhi the target of their operations.

After a nine-year deputation in the Central Bureau of Investigation (CBI), on my return to the Delhi Police in 2002, I had the privilege of heading the Special Cell for a couple of years. Pramod Kushwaha was an ACP posted with me and was a great asset—he was self-motivated, kept a low profile and was a commendable detective. Before joining the police, he had worked as a computer scientist at a premier research organization of the Government of India. His IT and software skills added considerable value to the cell. He used his cyber expertise—a skill that not many police officers have—to his advantage, solving many a case and busting many a terror group, chiefly on account of this skill. The email address he had chanced upon in Kashmir could—if luck was on our side—unravel a treasure trove of intelligence on terror and terrorists.

On his return to Delhi from Kashmir, Pramod, the thirty-five-year-old with only eight years of experience in policing, began working on the email ID he had noted while in Kashmir. The ID—rashid32XXXX@hotmail.com— belonged to one of the contacts of the slain terrorist, and curiously, its IP address was in Delhi. (For the uninitiated, an IP address, or Internet Protocol address, is a numerical label attached to each device connected to a computer network that uses the protocol for communication. An IP address serves two principal functions: host or network interface identification and location addressing. Put simply, it gives the location and address of an email sender.)

Further, this email ID was being used from IP addresses traced to different cyber cafés in Delhi. For instance, it was used from a cyber café in Paharganj on 1 February 2003, Daryaganj on 3 February, Moti Bagh on 7 February and so on. This discovery alarmed us, as it suggested that either an acquaintance or an associate of the terrorist killed by the BSF in Kashmir was in Delhi. But, why would such a person change his location so frequently to send emails, unless, we reasoned, he had some evil design. This called for immediate action, given the security scenario in the country at the time.

Since I was his immediate superior, Pramod brought his discoveries to my attention. I asked him to map the locations of the cyber cafés from where such emails were being sent.

A certain pattern emerged on conducting this exercise. The cyber cafés were located mostly in and around central Delhi.

We deployed several police teams in the vicinity of the cafés that had been mapped out. Additionally, our men went to each of these cafés posing as regular customers and planted software in their computers using floppy discs (still used in those days) to feed in 'hot words' such as football, chachaji, neha, stupa, love you, etc. (the reason these words were chosen will become clear later in the chapter) so that in the event that an email containing such words was detected, a message would immediately be sent to Pramod's phone from the computer used for receiving or sending such an email. Pramod, in turn, would direct the team located nearest to the café to check who was using the café's computers and pick up the person concerned. Though the cyber cafés were far too many and the police teams comparatively fewer, on a couple of occasions, our men came close to nabbing suspects, missing them only by a couple of minutes.

At this stage of the operation, something farcical, and what some readers may consider bizarre, happened. We celebrate Delhi Police Day on 16 February every year to mark the separation of our force from the erstwhile undivided Punjab Police to become an independent entity under the Government of India in 1948. The most important part of the celebrations is a ceremonial parade for which officers and men are drawn from different units of the Delhi Police. Pramod was also called to be a part of the parade as a gazetted officer leading a company of men. Since he was in the middle of an important operation involving a likely terror attack, I met the senior officer who was in charge of organizing the parade. Given the seriousness of the investigation at hand, Pramod could easily have been spared and another officer taken in his place. However, the officer—a senior of mine—would have none of it. The unfortunate consequence of the senior officer's adamant attitude was that during a crucial phase of the operation, Pramod was actually on parade. An alert that he received on 5 February while on parade could have resulted in the netting of a terrorist.

It is often the case that one unit of the police does not comprehend the significance of the work being done by another unit. Or, sometimes, an officer heading one unit, out of envy, creates hurdles in the way of the success of an officer in charge of another unit. But, most of the time, routine police activity and administrative duties come in the way of more serious, urgent and time-sensitive work. The fact of the matter was that the ACP was not where he ought to have been at a critical moment in the operation, thanks to the unreasonable stubbornness of a senior officer.

To get back to our story and the alarming emails we had chanced upon, another commonality was seen in the content of the emails being exchanged. The emails were made to appear as if they were love letters in English. The actual communication between the sender and the receiver, written in Roman Hindustani, was hidden in the midst of the mail. For instance, an email dated 11 February from rashid32XXXX@hotmail.com to stupaXX@hotmail.com read:

My darling I am coming to you soon. Please wait for me. It will not be long before we get married. You will come to me and I will come to you in your arms. Please

take me and keep me forever. *Dear brother Muzammil, salam wale kum, aapka message mila. Main us aadmi se mil loonga. Uska number abhi switch off hai. Thodi der me phir try karta hoon. Kaam ke baad aapko message bhejta hoon, Aapka bhai* [I have received your message. I shall meet that man. His phone is currently switched off. I shall try again after some time. After completing the task I shall inform you, your brother.] Thank you so much for the work. I am very happy that we are together and that we will stay together for the rest of our life. Nobody can separate us and we are one for all time.
(The English translation of the actual message written in Hindustani is within brackets.)

Another email dated 7 February from rashid32XXXX@ hotmail.com to stupaXX@hotmail.com read:

My dear darling I am so happy that you love me and you are made for me. You also know that I love you and that you are most important to me in this world. *Dear brother Muzzamil salam wale kum unko maine tehraa diya hai. Yeh college wala ilaqa hai. Bhir bhar main hai. Sab thik hai. Aur koi baat hogi to message bhej dena. Chachaji ko salaam arz karna, aapka bhai* [I have given him thirteen, I have put him up somewhere. This is an area full of colleges and there is a lot of activity here. Everything else is fine. If anything important comes up, I will let you know.] I love you and you love me. I will die if you are not in my life. I will get flowers for you everyday. I will give you lot of love.'

The contents of four other emails sent earlier—dated 28 January, 1 February, 3 February and 5 February 2003—from four different cyber cafés were more or less in the same vein. However, veiled mention of money transfers, hiring of hiding places and references to one 'chachaji' (who in all probability was Zakiur Rehman Lakhvi, a top leader of LeT and the supreme commander of operations in Kashmir) were worrisome. Indications of an imminent terror attack in or around Delhi seemed concealed in these messages. The idea behind this tactic seemed to be that if the emails were intercepted, they could be passed over as innocuous love letters—a modus operandi often adopted by terror groups.

* * *

Before proceeding with the story, a word or two about Lashkar-e-Taiba—which means army of the pure—and its top leader Zakiur Rehman Lakhvi, presumably the mastermind behind the terror plan.

LeT is a deadly militant group, operating mainly from Pakistan. Some of its stated objectives are to 'liberate' Muslims residing in 'Indian Kashmir' and to bleed India through a 'thousand cuts' caused by terror attacks. Founded in 1987 by Hafiz Saeed et al. with funding from Osama bin Laden, its headquarters are in Muridke near Lahore. The attack on the Indian Parliament in 2001 and the Mumbai attacks of 2008 are believed to have been executed by LeT. The group has been declared a terrorist organization by the US, the UK, Australia, Russia and by the United Nations in 2008. It is widely believed that the LeT enjoys the patronage of Pakistan's main intelligence agency, the Inter-Services Intelligence (ISI).

Zakiur Rehman Lakhvi was the mastermind of the 2008 terror attacks in Mumbai and figures prominently on India's most wanted list. His name figured in the confession of Ajmal Kasab, who was the only terrorist captured alive by the Mumbai Police following the Mumbai attacks. Lakhvi is referred to as 'chachaji' in Lashkar circles.

Now to get back to our story of February 2003. What confirmed our fears of an imminent terror attack was an email we intercepted on 13 February, originating from stupaXX@hotmail.com and sent to a new email ID, nehasingh1XX2@hotmail.com, which came to our notice for the first time. It read:

neha dear, *salaam wale kum, allah aapki hifazat karega, aap aur bhai apne kaam par lage raho* before 15/2/2003 *ko aapke shahar mein taariq usko lekar aapke pass aa jayega. Football ka kya karna hai aap behtar jaante ho. Match ke baad aap mujhey message de dena. Koi baat ho to 1.. ke zariye message bhejna aur online ho jaana. Aapka bhai M.*
[Neha dear, peace unto you, God will take care of you. You and others keep doing your work. Before 15 February 2003 Tariq will reach where you are along with him. You know better what needs to be done with the football. Please message me once the match is over. If there is any message please send it through 1..]

The '1..' at the end of the message in all probability meant 001, which perhaps implied that messages should be routed through the US, the calling code for which is 001.

The mention of 'football', which could be a code word for a bomb or a lethal weapon, and a 'match' after which the sender desired to be informed, set alarm bells ringing.

The next email we intercepted was sent on the same date, 13 February, twenty-seven minutes later. It read as follows:

> *Rashid bhai*, AOA[*], *Aapke zimme hai. Wahan sab kuch match ki tareekh fix hone tak players ka khayal rakhna. Aapke zimme hai. Koi baat hogi toh kya karna hai aap achi tarah jaante ho.* Zaid.
> [Rashid brother, the mission is your responsibility, until such time that the date of the match is not fixed, you have to take care of the players. This too is your responsibility. You know what needs to be done if anything goes wrong. Zaid.]

The above-mentioned message came from chachoji@hotmail.com and was sent to rashid32XXXX@hotmail.com. Our guess, as already mentioned, was that 'Chachoji' was none other than Zakiur Rehman Lakhvi.

The email clearly implied that a plan for a terrorist attack, masterminded by Zakiur Rehman Lakhvi, was afoot. Our apprehension was further strengthened by an email we intercepted the following day (14 February), again from chachoji@hotmail.com to rashid32XXXX@hotmail.com. It read:

---

[*] In all likelihood, AOA is an acronym for Allah-hu-Akbar (Allah is great).

Dear Rashid,
AOA. *Match ka date fix ho gaya hai. World cup ka final
25 ko tay hua hai. Time wahi hai match ka.* Best of luck.
Zaid.
[Dear Rashid, Allah is great. The date for the match is
fixed. The World Cup final is on 25 February. Time of
the match is the same. Best of luck. Zaid.]

The originating IP address was of Islamabad, Pakistan.

Besides informing my immediate superior, I took his
permission to inform the central intelligence agency we
usually worked with on such operations. When notified,
some in the agency were incredulous and thought we had
cooked it all up. Rather than take follow-up action on the
input, every effort was made to prove it was a hoax—a clear
example of inter-agency rivalry. How could the lowly local
police come up with such pinpointed intelligence, and that
too involving an imminent terror attack by a Pak-based
terror group, when it was the primary responsibility of the
central intelligence agency? That, I guess, was the thinking
of our colleagues in the intelligence outfit. Fortunately,
some other key officers in the agency, who had faith in us,
were impressed with the quality of cyber work done based
on what appeared to be an innocuous bit of information
collected in Kashmir. After a few initial hiccups, everyone
in the agency felt adequately alarmed and began to work
feverishly on the case.

The next email was again from Chachoji to Rashid, sent
on 17 February, originating from an IP address in Islamabad,
Pakistan. It stated:

Match ki jagah fix ho gayi hai .05 .000 .00 .05.7.03 .7
.0 .4 -7
*Sabko bol de ki ground dekh lein. Players ko practice
karna hai.*
[The venue for the match has been fixed. ------CODED
MESSAGE---------Please tell everyone to see the site
and the players must have a dry run.]

Earlier, Chachoji was sending emails from a computer with
an IP address based in Islamabad. But this email, dated
17 February, came from an IP address in Peshawar.

Curiously, the next email was sent on 18 February from
a new ID. It was from puranamakan@hotmail.com and
addressed to birthdXXX@hotmail.com. The originating
IP address was again in Peshawar. This time the email was
entirely in code. It read:

.7 .02 .5 .7 .02 .5 .6 .03 .002 .8 .1 .03 .06 .06 .7 .09 .07
.9 .004 .01 .09 .8 .5 .3 .003 .6 .9 .00 .09 .002 .9 .004
.03 .07 .9 .5 .0 .8 -5

Readers can imagine how anxious and worried we all were,
now that we were aware that a terror incident was imminent.
What made matters worse for us was that the planners, who
were shifting their location from one place in Pakistan to
another, had conveyed the location of the terror strike in a
coded message to the executors who were already in Delhi.
And, here we were, informed yet ignorant. Delhi was about
to be hit, innumerable lives would be lost, and the unit of the
Delhi Police—the Special Cell—meant to prevent and detect

terror strikes, although aware that an attack was imminent, was clueless of the details because it couldn't crack a code.

Various cryptographers based in Delhi were contacted. Some were in the armed forces, a few others worked in government research organizations, some were in universities and so on. Everyone contacted began to work on the code, but no one was able to crack it quickly. The intelligence agency we were collaborating with procured decoding software and computers overnight in an attempt to crack the code but to no avail.

The next email that came was on 19 February, again from chachoji@hotmail.com to rashid32XXXX@hotmail. com. It read:

Dear Rashid
Ek naya ID bana lo. Yahin par mujhko iss ID par mail karo. .002 .01 .004 .7 .000 .7 .07 .07 .7 .000 -7
Zaid.
[Dear Rashid, please make a new email ID. Then mail me on my present ID. -------CODED MESSAGE-----------
Zaid.]

This email was followed by another one sent a little over an hour later, at 11.46 a.m., from chachoji@hotmail.com to rashid32XXXX@hotmail.com stating:

Dear Rashid *naya id yah par nahi hot par hai aap bhi hot par bana lena aur neha ko bhi naya wala de dena aur bolna who bhee naya bana kar mail kare.* Zaid.
[Dear Rashid, the new ID is not on yah but is on hot. You too make your ID on hot and tell Neha to do

likewise. You both should mail me on my new ID so
created.]

It was not difficult to guess that 'yah' referred to yahoo and
'hot' to hotmail.

Since the code had not been cracked, the first message was
Greek to us. We felt like headless chickens running around
trying to decipher the code. There was a gnawing feeling in
the pit of my stomach telling me that disaster was about to
strike and we would certainly be hanged for it. Pramod went
to the extent of contacting a friend of his based in the US, who
worked for a cryptography company, to help us on an urgent
basis. The company quoted a price for the job, which was
prohibitive but worthwhile considering that many innocent
lives were in danger and national prestige was at stake. I met
my superior and informed him of the conundrum we were
in and the requirement of money in foreign exchange to be
paid abroad. My boss expressed his inability to be of any help
as the matter required approvals from various levels of the
Government of India and that too in a very short time.

At this hopeless juncture, when all seemed lost,
something providential happened. On 19 February, when we
were clueless, out of our depth and running out of time, a
saviour arrived on the scene in late afternoon. He was neither
a cop nor a computer whiz-kid nor a cryptologist. He was an
unemployed youth who had come looking for a job in Delhi.
He had nowhere to go except to Pramod, who had been his
senior in school. Vivek Thakur was his name. Vivek could
sense that things weren't right with his schoolmate, who had
anxiety writ large on his face. Vivek inquired what the matter

was. Without giving him any background information, Pramod told him that he was struggling with an encrypted message that could not be deciphered. On Vivek's request, Pramod shared the coded messages with him. Thereafter, Pramod left the office to seek help from diverse sources to decode the messages.

After a couple of hours, Pramod returned to his office, drained after what he felt was another wasted day of fruitless work. He found Vivek still sitting on the visitor's couch with pen and paper, working on the code. Pramod expressed his surprise on seeing him. Vivek looked up at him and said: 'Sir, I think I should be able to crack it.' Pramod brushed him aside saying a job was not done until it was done. Vivek, however, persevered with the code, mindless of Pramod's dismissive comment.

At this point, I sent Pramod a message that I wished to see him. I wanted to meet him to review the progress on the case.

The ACP left his office in Ashok Vihar for police headquarters, where my office was located. Vivek wanted to accompany him as he thought that at the end of the forty-minute drive to headquarters, he would have cracked the code. Reluctantly, Pramod agreed. Throughout the long drive amidst maddening traffic, the two friends did not exchange a word. Vivek remained drowned in thought, scribbling feverishly on a sheet of paper.

As they alighted near the stairs of the police headquarters, Vivek, in a eureka moment, let out a muted cry of triumph: 'Sir, I have cracked the code and it is very simple. It is a combination of binary and decimal systems that our maths teacher in school taught us.'

Pramod began to climb the stairs and heard Vivek out with incredulity. His friend explained that each letter of the English alphabet had been numbered from .0 to .9, starting with A. The tenth letter was numbered 00, with the decimal point shifting a digit to the left. So, A was numbered .0, B was .1, C was .2 and so on until J, which was numbered .9. With this method, K was not assigned the number .10 but instead .00, and L became .01, M was .02 and so on until T, which was numbered .09. Consequently, U was numbered .000, V was .001, W was .002, X was .003, Y was .004 and Z was .005.

To further clarify, I will put it down more elaborately. The code used for each letter of the alphabet is written below it:

A	B	C	D	E	F	G	H	I	J	K	L	M	N
0	.1	.2	.3	.4	.5	.6	.7	.8	.9	00	.01	.02	.03

O	P	Q	R	S	T	U	V	W	X	Y	Z
.04	.05	.06	.07	.08	.09	000	.001	.002	.003	.004	.005

In some emails, -5 or -7 was written at the end of the code. That meant that while decoding, the reader needed to count back those many letters. For instance, the email dated 17 February read:

'Dear Rashid, please make a new email ID. Then mail me on my present ID 002 .1 .004 .7 .09 .7 .07 .7 .000 – 7'.

Using this method, 002 was X, but if we counted back seven letters (as indicated by '-7' at the end of the message), it became P. The deciphered code therefore read 'purana makan'.

It was not surprising, therefore, that emails sent after 17 February originated from puranamakan@hotmail.com. The matching of this email ID confirmed that this indeed was the correct way to decode the messages.

While both schoolmates sat outside my office waiting for their turn to see me, Pramod once again made sure that the decoding formula worked out by Vivek was in order. When Pramod walked into my office he looked triumphant and relaxed. He explained the decoding methodology to me, and we were finally able to make sense of the coded emails. We then realized that India Gate was going to be the target of an attack, as mentioned in code in the email dated 15 February. The coded message, as stated earlier, was '.05 .000 .00 .05.7.03 .7 .0 .4 -7'. When decoded, it read 'India Gatx'. The last letter was a typo and 'x' was meant to be 'e'.

Therefore, the date for the terror attack was fixed as 25 February and the target was India Gate.

The email dated 18 February read 'Chacha bird will come two days before time Zak'.

Alarmingly, the next message, dated 21 February 2003, came from a new email ID, sundarbhXXXa_hindu@hotmail. com, and it was addressed to puranamakan@hotmail.com. It read:

Brother. *Assalam waley kum.*
Bhai main aaj hi Sri . . . se del.. aa gaya hun. Uss aadmi
se raabta karke aapko khabar karta hun.
Sundar
[Brother, God be with you. I have reached Del.. from
Sri . . . today. Once I have established contact with him
I will get back to you. Sundar]

This email was cause for further panic as it indicated that the plan was now in its final stages and someone had come from Srinagar to Delhi to ensure its successful execution.

The first thing I did was to inform my superior, the commissioner of police, Delhi. I suggested to him that the higher-ups in the government should be informed immediately, which he promptly did. Those readers who hail from Delhi and have visited India Gate would know that there was a time when a visitor could walk right up to the base of the monument. In the days before the new security system was imposed, milling crowds of men, women and children thronged the area around India Gate, along with ice cream and snack vendors. At any given point, a minimum of four to five thousand people were present there. From a terrorist group's viewpoint, what better target could there be than this, and that too at an iconic war memorial? The impact would have been as earth-shattering as the earlier attack on the Parliament House in 2001.

I clearly remember that on 22 February, I was summoned to a midnight meeting at the residence of the then home minister, L.K. Advani. The heads of various intelligence agencies, the home secretary and yours truly attended the meeting. I was asked to brief everyone present on the sequence of events and what needed to be done by the government. I showed to all present the encrypted messages, their decoded versions and the clear indications of an imminent terror strike at India Gate, as concealed in the emails exchanged. At the end of my presentation it was clear to all that there was an urgent need to deploy sufficient armed forces at India Gate. Without much ado, the decision was made to not take any chances and to make a show of our response. A detachment of the Indian Army was to be deployed immediately.

When the next day broke, early morning joggers on Rajpath were surprised to see army men wielding light machine guns stationed all around India Gate in full battle gear. A few light tanks were also stationed at strategic points for effect.

My sense is that the terrorists probably went to 'play' the 'World Cup', but seeing the army deployment there, quietly retreated. The exchange of emails stopped completely, which corroborated this inference. A major terror event had been averted and many lives saved. No one will know what effect such a terror attack would have had on Indo-Pak relations, which were fragile at the time in the aftermath of the Parliament House attack that had brought the armies of the two neighbours eyeball to eyeball.

At the end of this story, I can't help but get a bit platitudinous. Sometimes in life, what appears to be very complex and difficult to solve eventually turns out to be simple. The code that was being used by the terrorists in their emails appeared to be one such intractable riddle. Once the code was cracked, it suddenly looked simple and set us wondering why the best and most competent experts had not been able to crack it, despite having the latest software and hardware at their disposal. Or for that matter, why couldn't we crack it ourselves? But isn't this what happens in life all the time? Once we cross an obstacle that seems insurmountable, it looks simple in hindsight.

The arrival of a simple, unemployed youth—Vivek Thakur—on the scene when all seemed lost was providential. We may call it an act of God or pure serendipity. This story, in a way, tells us that sometimes people who would not warrant a second look are the people who truly matter.

ACP Pramod Kushwaha's visit to Kashmir, his meeting with the BSF officer, the sharing of the contents of a dead terrorist's diary between the two officers and the ability of Pramod to follow up on a stray email address were all strange but happy coincidences that cannot be understood and explained easily. There was possibly a higher force at work, determined to prevent mayhem at India Gate.

However, as a police officer, a regret lingers to date about this operation. It is that of not being able to apprehend any of the terrorists. I can console myself by thinking that perhaps this too was part of a larger design willed by the same higher force.

If a visitor to India Gate today is unable to approach the base of the war memorial for a closer look, she can curse us if she wants, now that I have let the cat out of the bag.

3

What the Doctor Ordered

The sixth of December 1992 was one of the darkest days in the history of modern India. On this fateful day, Babri Masjid, a sixteenth-century mosque reportedly built by the Mughal general Mir Baqi, was demolished by thousands of volunteers—known as kar sevaks. The kar sevaks are right-wing Hindu fundamentalists, and they believe that an ancient temple was razed to the ground to build the mosque. Demolition of the centuries-old structure breached the fragile amity between the Hindu and Muslim communities of India like few other events ever have. The circumstances leading up to this tragic event are worth a mention.

In Hindu tradition, the city of Ayodhya, in the north Indian state of Uttar Pradesh, is believed to be the birthplace of Lord Rama, the seventh incarnation of the Hindu god Vishnu. Some Hindus believe that Rama was born at the same site where Mir Baqi built the mosque after demolishing a temple of Rama, though historical evidence to support this contention is scarce. For over four centuries, both Hindus and Muslims used the site for religious purposes. Then in

1822, an official of the local court at Faizabad made the claim that the mosque stood on the site of a temple. Ever since then a dispute over the title of the land has festered between claimants of Hindu and Muslim communities and has led to discord between them from time to time.

In the 1980s the dispute came to a head when the Vishwa Hindu Parishad (VHP), a right-wing fundamentalist organization, began a campaign for the construction of a temple dedicated to Rama at the site of the mosque. On 6 December 1992, VHP organized a rally of roughly 1,50,000 kar sevaks that turned violent. The kar sevaks overwhelmed security forces and tore down the mosque. The demolition resulted in several months of communal riots between Hindus and Muslims, causing the death of at least 2000 people. Shock waves spread not only to different parts of the country but also to distant corners of the world, enraging the Muslim community and tarnishing the image of India as a secular and tolerant nation. Retaliatory violence against Hindus and their religious places was reported in Pakistan, Bangladesh and the Middle East.

In India, the repercussions—besides communal riots and killings—were seen in the increase in acts of terror, such as the deadly serial bombings in Mumbai on 12 March 1993 that claimed 279 lives, caused injuries to nearly 700 people and damage to property, both public and private, worth hundreds of crores of rupees. The divisive atmosphere in the country and the latent wrath in the Muslim community over the demolition of the mosque and the loss of lives during the riots were used as capital by the ISI, the notorious secret service agency of Pakistan, to foment trouble and terrorism.

The following story is of one of the many well-planned acts of terror whose genesis may be traced to the demolition of Babri Masjid.

* * *

In the early hours of 6 December 1993—the first anniversary of the demolition of Babri Masjid—shocking news of bombings in five trains were reported from different parts of the country, in which two passengers were killed and twenty-two injured. Railway property worth lakhs of rupees had been damaged. A sense of terror spread amongst railway workers and passengers alike, affecting normal train service for a long time. Details of the bombings are as follows:

At about 5.15 a.m. on 6 December 1993, a bomb kept under seat number 4 of coach C-7 of the Rajdhani Express en route to New Delhi from Mumbai Central exploded between the Indergarh and Amli stations in the Kota division of the Western Railway. The explosion resulted in five passengers being grievously injured, but fortunately there were no fatalities.

At 6 a.m. on the same day, a bomb kept under seat number 135 of coach D-1 of the Flying Queen Express, originating from Surat and going to Mumbai, exploded, causing grievous injury to one passenger and substantial damage to the railway coach.

A bomb planted in the toilet of the pantry car of the Rajdhani Express, running between New Delhi and Kolkata, exploded at 10.30 a.m. on the same day, between the Prempur and Karbigwan stations in the Allahabad division of the

Northern Railway. Two bearers in the pantry car sustained grievous injuries and the coach was badly damaged.

Two bombs were also planted in the Rajdhani Express originating from Kolkata and proceeding to New Delhi. One was placed in the toilet of coach C-6 and the other in the toilet of C-2. One of the bombs went off at 5 a.m., but the other was detected well in time for it to be defused at Bhaupur railway station in the Kanpur division of the Northern Railway.

A bomb placed under seat number 38 of coach 4895 of another prestigious train, the Andhra Pradesh Express, exploded at 7.05 a.m. The blast killed Ahmed Majid Ismail and Jeevan Jyoti—two hapless passengers travelling in the coach—demonstrating that when a terrorist's bomb explodes or his automatic rifle fires, neither the bomb nor the rifle pay heed to the religion or gender of their victims. In addition to these two fatalities, fifteen passengers sustained grievous injuries and serious damage was caused to the railway coach.

Yet another bomb placed in the Mumbai–Kurla Express was fortunately detected and defused in time on the same day.

Five criminal cases were registered at railway police stations: at Kota in Rajasthan, Kanpur (two cases) in Uttar Pradesh, Valsad in Gujarat and Malkajgiri in Andhra Pradesh. The police departments, assisted by their respective state crime branches, commenced investigations, but they were unable to make any headway. The Government of India, cognizant of the interstate nature of these crimes and their national importance, transferred the five cases to the CBI through two notifications dated 21 December and 28 December 1993. The then director of CBI, K. Vijaya Rama Rao, decided to entrust the investigation of these five cases to the nascent Special Task Force (STF) that had been constituted in the CBI only six months earlier.

* * *

The STF was created in May 1993, primarily to investigate the 12 March 1993 serial bombings in Mumbai. In the wake of these blasts and their catastrophic aftermath, several controversies had arisen related to the investigation of the case by the Mumbai Police Crime Branch. Even though the police had cracked the case and arrested several of the accused, allegations of links between some of the perpetrators and powerful politicians of the state, corruption and high-handedness on the part of the police, and the sheer scale of the crime with national and transnational ramifications led to a public outcry for the case to be transferred to the CBI.

The case came to the CBI on 19 November 1993 and we in the STF got busy scrutinizing the voluminous documents that came with the case files and figuring out what our course of action should be. There were several loose ends to be tied up, further investigations to be conducted and absconding accused to be arrested. I was the deputy inspector general (DIG) in charge of the case in the STF. As it usually happens in the government, when new units are created, they are formed using existing resources—both human and material—by withdrawing them from one branch or another. The number of hands given to you is small and so are other material resources such as office space or transport. In the midst of these teething troubles came the orders transferring the five serial train blast cases, which demanded investigative legwork all over the country.

Without losing our focus on the Mumbai blasts, we began the process of taking over the case files of the train bombings from the railway police of Uttar Pradesh, Andhra Pradesh, Rajasthan and Gujarat. Visits to the crime scenes and consultations with local police officers followed.

In the midst of all this, on 13 January 1994, K. Vijaya Rama Rao called me to his office in the North Block and directed me to proceed to Hyderabad. Apparently, an informant of an ACP of the Hyderabad police had secret information about the serial train blast cases that he wished to share with the CBI. There was a possibility that the tip-off would require a full-fledged operation in Mumbai. My immediate superior, Joint Director S. Sen, was asked to leave for Mumbai, while I flew to Hyderabad to meet the informant.

I reached Hyderabad at around 8 p.m. I was to stay in the local police mess, but I drove straight from the airport to the office of the ACP, who was a prominent member of the Anti-Terrorist Squad (ATS) in the Hyderabad Police. The real name of the ACP eludes me now, but I remember that he was popularly called Gabbar Singh. His colleagues, on account of his imposing height, build and rather villainous looks that belied his friendly disposition, had given him this moniker. It was a pleasure to meet him and exchange details of the work being done by our respective units, which led to an immediate kinship.

Soon the ACP sent for his informant and in walked a short and frail man in his mid-thirties. He was unkempt and rather smelly. Gabbar Singh introduced me to him saying that I was the CBI officer sent from Delhi to follow up on the information he had. I tried my best to make the informant feel at ease and soon he began to talk freely with me in his typical Hyderabadi Hindi. His conversation with me, still etched in my memory, went something like this: 'Sahib, *apne kuch jaante jo tumko batana kya?*' (Shall I tell you something that may be useful to you), he asked. When I said he may, he asked me, '*Kya aap* AP Express *ka bomb dhamaka* case *dekhte?*' (Are you looking into the AP Express blast case?) When I replied in the affirmative, he said, 'Bombay *me ek jagah hai Mominpura. Wahan ek* doctor *hai jiska naam apun ko nahee maloom. Par uska khairat ka ek hospital hai Mominpura mein. Woh* mastermind *hai, usko dhoondo, woh aap ko sab bata sakta hai.*' (There is a place in Mumbai called Mominpura where a Muslim doctor resides. He runs a charitable hospital but is the mastermind behind the blasts. Please look for him.)

The information was rather sketchy, but I had to make the most of it. The first logical step was to share it with my field officers in Mumbai. That would require the exchange of information in real time between Satish Jha—my able junior colleague and superintendent of police (SP) in Mumbai—and myself. Mobile telephony had not reached India as yet. To add to my woes, even the subscriber trunk dialling (STD) facility was not available on Gabbar Singh's office phone. (In those days, official telephones, whether at home or at work, were provided with the STD facility only if they were for the use of very senior-ranking officers. I also remember that a common practice to avoid the misuse of the facility was to keep the telephone instrument locked or to protect its use by means of a code that was known only to the officers.)

So, I booked a trunk call (as inter-city calls were then called) and passed the information on to Satish. Five years my junior, Satish was a hands-on police officer known for his investigative and operational skills and had been with me on several sensitive missions. He quickly collected his team of handpicked officers and decided to rope in the Mumbai Police, which was just as well. The residents of Mominpura, a sprawling shanty town where the suspect supposedly lived, formed a well-knit community and were not particularly appreciative of governmental agencies—least of all the police—intruding into their territory.

An advance party comprising Deputy Superintendent of Police (DSP) Pramod Mudbhatkal and Inspector Raman Tyagi first tried to locate the charitable hospital in Mominpura but drew a blank. Satish, heading the joint police team of STF and Mumbai Police, did not wish to carry out obtrusive inquiries for fear of crowds gathering and creating a law and order situation. He called me on Gabbar Singh's office number from a local STD booth in Mominpura to ask if the informant had shared any further information. The informant had by then given details of several landmarks, which I shared with Satish. He and his officers looked for them but could locate neither the charitable hospital nor the doctor's whereabouts.

By then it was well past midnight and the residents of Mominpura had retired for the day. Except for a few tea stalls and paan shops, all business establishments had closed. The streets were relatively deserted, with stray dogs barking at the alien policemen prowling the area. It had been hours since the search had started. A few passers-by had begun to cast suspicious glances at the CBI men, who were running out of time. Satish was losing patience and getting tense. At a street corner, he spotted a taxi parked with its driver sitting inside, waiting, perhaps, for his last customer before he called it a day. On an impulse, Satish asked the cabby if he knew of a charitable hospital in the neighbourhood as a close relative of his required immediate medical attention. The cabby asked if Satish was looking for the 'khairati' (charitable) hospital run by Dr Jalees Ansari. Satish, ignorant of the name of the man who ran the charitable hospital, took a chance and said yes. The cabby gave precise directions not only to the hospital but also to the chawl (shanty) where the doctor lived, which was on the floor above the hospital. Luckily for Satish, he offered to walk with him and point out the place.

As the cabby began to lock the car doors, Satish signalled Pramod and Raman to follow him but at a distance. The police officers felt they were finally in business. Adrenaline began to course through their veins and their hearts began to pound uncontrollably. They knew, almost instinctively, that their quarry was within sniffing distance, much like a predator on sighting its prey.

Satish and the cabby, with Pramod and Raman in tow, reached their destination in no time. The charitable hospital, with a prominent sign, stood right before them, and above it was a row of chawls, all almost identical and barely visible in the feeble light emanating from the municipal lamp posts nearby. Satish asked the cabby if he could do him one last favour. Could he accompany him to the doctor's chawl lest he knock on the wrong door? The cabby obliged, walking up the creaking stairs with him, down a narrow corridor and right up to the doctor's chawl. He knocked on the door, announcing that someone needed medical attention urgently.

A young boy, aged about fourteen, opened the ramshackle door of the shanty. Satish asked if Dr Ansari was at home. By then the bearded doctor, who was in his early forties, came to the door and asked Satish what the matter was. Satish engaged him in small talk about a non-existent patient in need of medical help, while his two officers walked right into the chawl. Before the doctor could object to the men walking uninvited into his house, they started to look underneath the scant furniture and rummage through the old, rusted trunks lying in the house. The doctor, enraged, began to curse at Satish and his men and ordered them to leave his house. Just then, an officer from Satish's team forced open a steel trunk in the loft of the living room and found weapons, detonators and wires inside. The discovery of arms and bomb-making material put paid to the doctor's protests.

The commotion at Dr Ansari's house had woken up his neighbours. Word of a police raid spread like wildfire, and a small crowd collected by the roadside, a flight below the doctor's chawl. The number of onlookers began to increase by the second. The police team realized that they were likely to be surrounded and overwhelmed. Satish sent a wireless message to the Mumbai Police control room, using the handset of the local police team escorting him, and asked for reinforcements. A fairly sizeable contingent of armed police arrived at the spot. Nonetheless, the crowd was agitated as Dr Ansari was a popular figure in his neighbourhood. As soon as the police team emerged with Dr Ansari from his chawl, the crowd started raising slogans against the cops. With great difficulty, the joint police team took Dr Ansari out from Mominpura to the STF office, located near the Sachivalaya in south Mumbai.

It was about 3 a.m. when Satish called to inform me of the developments. I was delighted that my team had succeeded in making its first big arrest in the case and had recovered weapons and bomb-making material. Calls were made to and fro between Mumbai and Hyderabad. Gabbar Singh's informant was pleased to learn that the information given by him had resulted in fruitful action.

It was close to 4 a.m. when I got to the police mess. In spite of being fatigued and sleep-deprived, I was euphoric with success. We had made a major breakthrough in a case that had seemed intractable until very recently. I don't know when I fell asleep.

I had barely slept a couple of hours when there was a knock on my door. It was an officer from the Hyderabad Police who informed me that the city's commissioner of police, H.J. Dora, had invited me to breakfast at his residence. Apparently, he too had received news of Dr Ansari's arrest—presumably from Gabbar Singh—and was keen to meet me.

Bleary-eyed and short on sleep, I reached the Dora residence where the commissioner greeted me warmly. This invitation to breakfast was in appreciation of the work we had done to arrest Dr Ansari. I was touched by his gesture and felt even more encouraged to take the case to its logical conclusion. Meeting Mr Dora was a dream come true for me since I had heard so much about him. He was a gutsy professional who called a spade a spade before his political masters, unmindful of the consequences. He was a true leader of men, suave and soft-spoken, the sort of cop they no longer make.

* * *

From the Dora residence I drove straight to the airport and took the first flight to Mumbai. Thanks to Mumbai traffic, the journey from the airport to south Mumbai took much longer than the flight from Hyderabad to Mumbai. By the time I arrived at the STF office, my colleagues had obtained the detainee's police remand.

As I walked into Satish's office, I saw Dr Ansari seated on a chair with three CBI officers sitting around him and interrogating him. My colleagues stood up to greet me as I walked in, and, in a dejected tone, one of them said, 'Sir, since morning the doctor has not uttered a word. He is even refusing to acknowledge that weapons and detonators were recovered from his house.'

On hearing this, I decided to try my luck at interrogating Dr Ansari. But the man didn't so much as blink. I felt at a loss as to what to do next. He was frail-looking, and the question of being tough on him didn't arise. As I sat looking at the doctor, I knew that I had to get him talking and soon. We had come this far, caught a man with weapons and detonators, but we needed to go further. We had to get the contours of Dr Ansari's conspiracy and follow up on them. And for this, we needed the doctor to open up. But, he was in no hurry to give in and proved to be a tough nut to crack.

Many emotions stirred within me and several thoughts crossed my mind. Almost instinctively, I addressed the detainee and said, 'Doctor, if I brought your holy book here, would you swear by it and say that you know nothing?' Dr Ansari froze and looked into my eyes meekly and helplessly. His face contorted and he burst into tears. He wept uncontrollably as his resolve to hold back what he knew broke on hearing mention of his holy book. Clearly, he was a deeply religious man, to the extent of being a fanatic. He could withstand the psychological pressures of a police interrogation; he could deal with being publicly shamed, as he had been the night before when he was whisked away by the police in the presence of his brethren; he could live with the prospect of his imminent separation from his family; but, under no circumstances could he swear by his holy book and lie. He kept crying and mumbling to himself inaudibly. I was tempted to hold him and comfort him but held myself back. The doctor gradually came to terms with himself. Slowly, he regained his composure and began to talk about himself, his radicalization, the coming together of a committed group of people and so on. He was blurting out information as if he wished to purge himself of the immense reservoir of emotions bottled up inside him. He spoke so freely and rapidly that it was difficult to keep pace with him while recording his copious disclosures in black and white. Such an outpouring was nothing new for us. Many a time, when a criminal breaks down during an interrogation, he no longer wishes to hold back any information. All he wants is to get rid of every last secret buried in his psyche and be at peace with himself. He cares little for the consequences of his confession. In the police lingo of north India this is alluded to as '*woh khul gaya*' (he has opened up).

Doctor Ansari poured his heart out and gave us the details of his life; how he had turned from being a benevolent physician to a radical fundamentalist and finally, a terrorist.

* * *

Jalees Ansari was born and raised in the Basti district of Uttar Pradesh. A bright student with dreams of becoming a doctor, he moved to Mumbai to study medicine. By dint of hard work, he made it to Sion Medical College and successfully earned his MBBS degree. He joined the public health department of the then Bombay Municipal Corporation in 1983. He got married soon after and settled down in Mominpura, one of the many predominantly Muslim shanty towns of Mumbai. Deeply religious by nature, he came under the influence of Ahl-e-Hadees, a religious movement started in north India in the mid-nineteenth century that believes in following Islam in its original and purest form. He would frequent only such mosques where Ahl-e-Haees followers congregated. Occasionally, clergy from other parts of India would visit these mosques and give fiery and provocative speeches on alleged atrocities committed against Muslims in Kashmir. Prominent amongst such speakers was Azam Ghauri, an Islamist from Karimnagar in Andhra Pradesh. He was a brilliant orator who had links with Naxalites and LeT. He had received extensive training in subversive activities in Pakistan and Afghanistan and was wanted for several crimes in Andhra Pradesh, including the murder of a senior police officer in Hyderabad.

Dr Ansari struck up a friendship with Ghauri and was deeply influenced by his radical views on seeking revenge on the Government of India and the majority community. During one of his visits to the Mominpura mosque in 1986–87, one Abdul Karim aka Tunda (a moniker given in some parts of north India to anyone with only one arm) accompanied Ghauri. An experienced and determined agent provocateur working for Pakistan's ISI, Tunda had plans to carry out terror attacks in and around Mumbai. He soon realized that Dr Ansari was the right person to collaborate with in this mission.

But before we continue with the story of their partnership, a word or two about Tunda. Born in an impoverished family in Delhi in 1943, he moved to his native village Pilakhuwa in the Ghaziabad district of Uttar Pradesh to study at a madrasa. From an early age he showed signs of religious fanaticism. In the wake of the Ram Janmabhoomi movement in India, he began his search for answers to the question why Muslims in India were doomed to be passive victims in the face of oppression by the majority community. In 1985, he was a witness to serious communal riots in his native village when he saw his relatives being burnt alive by mobs. Several Muslim-run shops and a mosque were targeted by the rampaging marauders. These events turned him into a rabid fundamentalist and easy prey for the ISI.

In 1993 he went to Pakistan and received training in LeT-run training camps. On his return, he was responsible for over forty bombings in India. He convinced Dr Ansari that mere discussions and proclamations on the problems of Muslims would do little good for the oppressed minority community and it was time to take some direct and decisive action. Tunda convinced the doctor to learn the use of firearms and the technique of making bombs. The doctor wanted to know where he could get such training. Tunda was ready to teach him bomb-making then and there. He had brought with him explosive material, detonators, timers, etc. The doctor, who had until then examined patients suffering from physiological ailments and helped them with cures, was persuaded in no time to learn bomb-making. The doctor was ready to kill innocent people with his new skills, unmindful of what his medical education had prepared him for. The metamorphosis the good doctor had undergone amazed Jalees Ansari himself. Dr Jekyll had turned into Mr Hyde.

The coming together of Azam Ghauri, Abdul Karim Tunda and Dr Jalees Ansari was a meeting of three evil and dangerous minds. Both Ansari and his mentor Tunda kept in touch and soon the latter sent fresh supplies of explosive material to Ansari. In the interim, Ansari had collected a small team of like-minded people, all based in Mumbai, all ready to do his bidding. Tunda came down to Mumbai and made bombs at Dr Ansari's residence, which the doctor and three of his compatriots—Saleem, Bachchu and Raees—planted in five gurdwaras in Andheri, Khar, Sion, Haliwada and CST station to incite communal disaffection amongst Sikhs. This was the first criminal activity the doctor had indulged in. There was no looking back for him thereafter. He and his team members, all belonging to the Ahl-e-Hadees school of thought, now had expertise in making and planting bombs. The year was 1989.

* * *

Dr Ansari's campaign against the majority community and the establishment in general came to a head after December 1992, when the Babri Masjid was demolished. Sensing the strong anti-Hindu feeling amongst the Muslims, Ahl-e-Hadees members collected arms, ammunition and explosives in ample quantities to give further impetus to their campaign.

After targeting the gurdwaras, Ansari's team targeted several police station premises in Mumbai, the Shiv Sena office and the election office of Dr Datta Samant (a prominent labour leader). A few explosions caused fatalities, but the group eluded law enforcement agencies and the intelligence fraternity of the country. By then prosperous Muslim benefactors had begun to come forward to finance the criminal activities of the doctor and his team.

During this period, Ansari met one Ashfaque Khan at the office of a close relative. Ashfaque was a mining contractor in Dausa, Rajasthan, and he and Ansari hit it off well. Ashfaque took it upon himself to divert explosive material from government supplies given to him for mining work. The doctor went to Dausa, where he received enough explosive material from Ashfaque to keep him in business for a long time.

By the middle of 1993, Dr Ansari's team was going from strength to strength. The terror module was planting bombs further afield from Mumbai in places such as Hyderabad and Gulbarga in Karnataka. Thanks to Tunda, Dr Ansari's circle of associates had assumed a pan-Indian character. Tunda had introduced him to prominent Ahl-e-Hadees members such as Dr Habib of Rae Bareli and Dr Jamal Alvi of Lucknow.

In August 1993, the leading lights of Ahl-e-Hadees met at Dr Alvi's residence in Lucknow. It was decided to step up the activities of the group and call it 'Crush India Force'. Another meeting was held in September 1993, again in Lucknow, during which it was decided to undertake dramatic action on the first anniversary of the demolition of Babri Masjid. It was Dr Ansari who proposed that prestigious trains such as the Rajdhani Express and the Andhra Pradesh Express should be targeted to strike at the elite class of society travelling in such trains, so that the government felt the heat of their action.

In pursuance of this conspiracy, different modules were created to execute six blasts, which would take place in the Rajdhani Express from Delhi to Kolkata, the Rajdhani Express from Kolkata to New Delhi, the Andhra Pradesh Express from Hyderabad to New Delhi, the Flying Queen from Surat to Mumbai and the Mumbai–Kurla Express. It was unanimously decided that the explosions would go off in the early hours of 6 December 1993 (the first anniversary of the Babri Masjid demolition). Bombs were assembled at the residence of Dr Ansari, then taken by different sub-modules to various locations where the bombers stayed at cheap hotels under fake names. They reserved seats under assumed identities, boarded the trains as planned and planted the bombs minutes before getting off at predetermined stations. The timers of the bombs were set to detonate between 5 a.m. and 10.30 a.m.

Five of the six bombs went off as planned. The sixth bomb, which was placed in the Mumbai–Kurla Express, was detected in time and defused without causing any harm.

With the news of each explosion, panic spread amongst train passengers and railway authorities alike. Trains were stopped at the first available stations—often nondescript and remote with little infrastructure—and searched by railway police. A few passengers disembarked from their trains and ran for safety. Railway traffic and train schedules went haywire and took days to normalize. Further, as information poured in from remote railway police stations through the nationwide police wireless network (POLNET), a sense of alarm gripped state and government authorities, including police and intelligence agencies. Uncomfortable questions were directed at several people in positions of authority, demanding explanations for the intelligence failure. Indeed, a nationwide terror network had struck at different locations in a well-orchestrated attack without anyone getting even a whiff of either the likelihood of these strikes or the identities of the perpetrators. Some people in government, especially in the intelligence agencies—both state and Central—owed the people an explanation.

This incident, coupled with earlier blasts perpetrated by the same group, called into question the authorities' claim of having resolved the serial bomb blast cases that had occurred only months earlier in March 1993, further adding to the sense of fear and panic. Many detractors of Mumbai Police contended that if the real perpetrators of the crime had been arrested or identified, how were blasts still occurring in and around Mumbai? The significance of the date of the attacks—6 December 1993—was not lost on anyone.

* * *

After the arrest of Dr Ansari and the disclosures made by him, we in the STF conducted simultaneous raids across

the country in which fifteen other associates were either
arrested or identified. These operations were conducted in
close coordination with the local police of Lucknow and Rae
Bareli in Uttar Pradesh, the Dausa Police in Rajasthan and
the Gulbarga Police in Karnataka. During the investigation,
evidence such as train reservation forms, entries and signatures
in hotel registers, eyewitness accounts, confessions recorded
under the Terrorist and Disruptive Activities (Prevention) Act
(referred to as TADA), and explosive material and weapons
from the individuals accused were collected. A charge sheet
was filed in August 1994 in a TADA court in Ajmer. Earlier,
all the bomb blast cases had been clubbed together and
were being investigated by us as a single case. The trial of
this case dragged on for nearly ten years and the final court
order came on 28 February 2004, convicting all accused and
sentencing them to life imprisonment.* O.P. Chhatwal, my
SP in Delhi, played a major role in marshalling the evidence,
presenting it in court and securing the convictions. The
conviction of all fifteen accused individuals with sentences to
life imprisonment in a single case was a rare occurrence in the
history of the Indian police.

Dr Ansari and his co-conspirators are today in Ajmer
Central Jail serving their life sentences. On 6 April 2000,
Azam Ghauri, one of the three masterminds, was killed in an
encounter with Hyderabad Police in Jagtiyal, now in Telangana
state. Seventeen years after the killing of Azam Ghauri, the
Delhi Police arrested the third mastermind, Abdul Karim

---

*   Special TADA court of Ajmer order dated 28 February 2004
     in *CBI vs. Mohd. Jalees Ansari and Others.*

Tunda, at the Indo-Nepal border on 16 August 2017. He is currently lodged in Ajmer Jail and is still undergoing trial in the serial train blast cases of 6 December 1993.

This was one of the major cases I was associated with during my nine-year stint in the CBI. The unearthing of the countrywide network of a terror group, whose existence was, until then, unknown to any state police force or to any intelligence agency, has been a matter of great personal satisfaction. Besides the resolution of the serial train blast cases, the mystery behind over forty intermittent bomb blasts in and around Mumbai, including the blasts at gurdwaras and police stations, was solved. A deadly terror group had been identified and put away and scores of people saved from deadly terror attacks.

4

Devil's Advocate

I was posted as the director general of prisons, Delhi, on 22 November 2010. Having served all my years with the police force in mainstream assignments, this posting came as a shock, at least initially. A bit of unsavoury police politics was behind it, but I will not waste my breath over it here. As it turned out, my stint in the new job turned out to be a memorable and fulfilling tenure. This story is one of many from my Tihar days.

Delhi prisons are commonly referred to as Tihar Jail. However, what is not commonly known is that it is not one jail, but consists of ten jails—numbered one to ten—located in one complex in what was once an urban village called Tihar. Another prison complex exists in Rohini, in far west Delhi, which is also an integral part of the prisons department of the capital. In 2016, five years after I left the prisons department, another prison complex, comprising six jails, became operational at Mandoli in north-east Delhi, bordering Uttar Pradesh.

It may be of some interest for a reader that besides the director general, who is a senior officer from the Indian Police Service (IPS), no other staff member serving in the jail is from the police. Therefore, when an IPS officer joins at the senior-most position in the prisons department, he is the sole policeman there and finds himself 'alone' in an unfamiliar environment. The discipline, regimentation and camaraderie found in the police are missing. More importantly, having spent his entire professional life pursuing and putting away offenders, he is suddenly supervising their correctional and reformation work—an occupation he is clueless about. The assignment thus is not particularly coveted and often considered a 'punishment' posting. This is true not only of Delhi but most other states in India as well.

Readers may further like to know a bit about the hierarchical structure of the jail staff. Under the director general, who heads the prisons department, a deputy inspector general of prisons serves as the second in command. Under them, a superintendent heads the administration of a jail. A deputy superintendent, assistant superintendents and head wardens followed by jail wardens assist the jail superintendent.

A couple of days after taking over, I decided to pay a visit to all the jails in the Tihar complex. The visit began from jail number two, where convicts sentenced to imprisonment for ten years or more were lodged. I must confess that before I stepped in, I was full of trepidation. Was I walking into hell on earth? How would the inmates react on seeing me? Would I be booed or jeered at by them? All manner of fears haunted me.

Escorted by jail staff, I entered jail number two and the sight I beheld was in sharp contrast to what I was expecting. The sprawling campus was a vast space of lush green lawns with squeaky-clean pathways flanked by tall trees. To my right, soon after the entry point, was a flour mill where wheat was being crushed to make flour. The staff led me in and I stood there for a few minutes to observe the proceedings. Convicts, all dressed in their immaculate white uniforms, were running the unit in unison. They greeted me respectfully and then went about doing their jobs as the crushing machine was operational and could not be left unattended. Each inmate was engrossed in his work, and if at all they spoke to one another, it was in low, hushed whispers.

As I stepped out, the only sound one could clearly hear in the campus was the song of birds chirping in the background.

I walked on and was ushered into the garment-making section of the prison. Mannequins stood outside the section dressed in outfits designed and stitched by inmates who worked with devotion on their machines or handlooms. The garments made by the inmates were novel in their design and of excellent quality. It looked like a fashion outlet in busy Karol Bagh, except for the absence of milling crowds.

Then there was the next big surprise: the prison bakery. I entered the huge baking hall and found the prisoners wearing white chef's hats, transparent gloves and face masks, skilfully kneading dough, cutting out cookies, stuffing patties and baking bread, pastries and cakes. The floor of the hall was spotless, and the machines and utensils shining clean. I thought to myself that the standards of hygiene here would easily put to shame those of the best restaurants and five-star hotels of the city! I was informed that all products made in the jail premises were retailed under the brand name TJ's (Tihar Jail's) and the brand had an impressive turnover with the potential to rise manifold. It was pleasing to know that every inmate was paid a daily wage, which they could spend on themselves or send home for the upkeep of their family.

I next visited the library, painting studio, hair salon and a medical room. I also saw convicts playing cricket in white flannels in a reasonably sized, open-air stadium. Someone in my entourage informed me that the jail had a well-established team called Tihar 11, which played club-level matches with outside teams.

The preconceived notion of a prison, with convicts in their striped black and white uniforms hammering at rocks, controlled by ruthless jail staff, disappeared. The place felt more like a retreat, an ashram—a serene expanse of tranquillity and peace.

I also ran into convicts whom I recognized from my long years in the Delhi Police and the CBI. Many had been arrested by police teams working under me. I saw a person who suffered from dwarfism, whom I immediately recognized. He was Tantrey, member of a terrorist outfit we had busted when I was joint commissioner of the Special Cell of the Delhi Police. He was working on a sewing machine and it was amusing to see how he avoided making eye contact with me and pretended to focus on his job.

Another person I took note of was a tall, muscular, broad-shouldered middle-aged man with a spring in his gait, who walked several yards ahead of me and the jail staff escorting me. Dressed in a white shirt, white trousers and white canvas shoes, he strutted around as if he owned the jail. I took him to be a jail employee walking with me to provide security. Occasionally, he would tick off an inmate here and a jail warden there.

So taken up was I by his personality that I inquired of the jail superintendent who he was. The jail superintendent whispered in my ear that he was a convicted murderer. A little later, during my walk-around, out of sheer curiosity, I inquired, 'Whose murder was he involved in?'

Someone from my entourage replied, 'Sir, he killed an advocate.'

Though anxious to know more details, I restrained the urge to ask further questions and waited for an opportune moment.

I visited the living quarters—or wards—where inmates were lodged. Though overcrowded, they were reasonably neat and clean. After I spoke to a few inmates, I was taken to the jail kitchen, where chefs from amongst the inmates were cooking food for over a thousand fellow convicts. Much like what I had seen in the prison bakery, the cooks wore caps and gloves and went about their jobs in a clockwork fashion, churning out rotis on giant tawas at a frenetic pace. The superintendent requested me to taste the food and record my comments in the inspection register. A bite of roti taken with dal and sabzi tasted sublime. I dutifully recorded my complimentary inspection note, heaping praise on the prisoner chefs.

Soon the inspection was over and my entourage was ushered to a garden within the jail premises for tea and refreshments. Plastic chairs and tables were laid out neatly on a manicured lawn surrounded by rows of flowers in bloom, overhanging trees and an artificial lake full of geese. Alongside was a flock of pigeons feeding merrily under the setting sun. I was told by the gardener that the pigeons were set free early every morning and by evening they returned to their allotted pigeonholes without fail. The sylvan surroundings belied the fact that we were sitting in a jail and being served tea by people convicted of heinous offences.

By now, I was totally at ease. The convicts, when seen in flesh and blood inside a jail, were the antithesis of whatever we imagine them to be. They were calm, docile and seemed at peace with themselves. I felt the time was right to ask further questions about the tall and muscular man who had led us all the way through my inspection.

I turned to the superintendent and inquired, 'Whom did the man who walked ahead of us murder?'

The superintendent was not too sure. His deputy came to his help. 'Sir, he was an advocate who lived in Model Town.'

I wanted to know more because by now several bells were ringing in my head.

'What was the advocate's name?' I asked impatiently.

His reply hit me like the proverbial bolt from the blue, leaving me shaken.

'Sir, his name was Bawa Gurcharan Singh.'

'Oh my god, is that so?' I blurted involuntarily.

I had known Bawa Gurcharan Singh, an eminent advocate, only too well. Not only had I known him, I was deeply indebted to him. Nearly twenty years ago he had come to my rescue when I faced trying times fighting a public interest litigation (PIL) filed against my officers and myself. The circumstances were such that no other advocate was willing to take our brief and argue our case in the Delhi High Court. But, more about that later.

I beckoned the tall man over and asked him, 'Did you kill Bawa Gurcharan Singh?'

'Yes, sir,' he said with a straight face.

'What is your name?'

'Sir, Manjeet Singh.'

Even though the incident had taken place nearly twenty years ago, I remembered some facts of the case.

'You were not alone when this happened. There was someone else with you.'

'Sir, there were two other people with me.'

'Where is the main guy?'

'Sir, I was the main guy. It was I who pulled the trigger. The Mathura Police killed my accomplice Brij Mohan in an encounter later.'

This again rang a bell and memories came rushing in. A close relative of a senior colleague (a former commissioner of the Mumbai Police) was kidnapped from his home in Jhansi in August 1991 and kept hostage. The ransom demanded was staggering and the hostage's family was not in a position to pay it. My colleague asked me to help. He had come to know that Shailendra Sagar, the senior superintendent of police (SSP), Jhansi, was my batchmate. I called up Shailendra who, of course, was aware of the case and said he was doing his best. Through good luck and some smart sleuthing, not only did Sagar rescue the hostage, but he also killed the kidnapper

Brij Mohan Sharma in a fierce encounter that took place in a sugar cane field in Mathura.

* * *

I crossed paths with Gurcharan Singh under circumstances that were rather convoluted. To explain them I need to give a bit of background on some of the momentous events that took place in our country in the 1970s, '80s and '90s. One such event was the mass agitation against the Mandal Commission recommendations.

The Mandal Commission or the Socially Backward Classes Commission was established on 1 January 1979 by the Janata Party government under Prime Minister Charan Singh. Its aim was to identify the 'socially or economically backward classes' of India. B.P. Mandal, an Indian parliamentarian, headed the commission to consider the question of reservation for such categories of people who had suffered for centuries on account of caste discrimination. By using eleven social, economic and educational indicators to determine backwardness, the commission in 1980 submitted its report recommending that a new category of the Indian population should be identified, namely, Other Backward Classes (OBC), which comprised 51 per cent of India's population. The commission further recommended that 27 per cent of jobs under the Central government and public sector undertakings should be reserved for OBCs, thereby making the total percentage of reservations a whopping 49 per cent of government jobs.

The commission's recommendations were pending implementation for about seven years when in August 1990 the Janata Dal government led by V.P. Singh declared its intent to implement them.

The criticism and reaction to the proposed implementation were sharp and severe. Student protests were particularly serious and widespread. The protests started in Delhi University and spread all over the country. At the time I was serving as deputy commissioner of police, south district, in Delhi. And it so happened that the area under my jurisdiction became the epicentre of these protests.

On 19 September 1990, students of Deshbandhu College and Bhagat Singh College—both under my jurisdiction—were protesting by throwing brickbats at public transport and blocking traffic. I reached the spot with police reserves and tried to control the mob. In our presence, Rajeev Goswami, a student of Deshbandhu College, tried to commit self-immolation in protest against the government's intent to implement the Mandal Commission's recommendations. My men managed to save him by quickly putting a blanket over him. He was rushed to the burns ward of Safdarjung Hospital where he fought a brave battle for his life and, fortuitously, survived. Goswami became the face of the agitation against the Mandal Commission, and his action sparked a series of self-immolation bids by other upper-caste college students, who strongly disputed the commission's recommendations as they found them to be unjust and biased against the deserving.

* * *

Before grade separators and an interchange came up at the All India Institute of Medical Sciences (AIIMS) intersection, where Ring Road and Sri Aurobindo Marg cross each other, it was not only one of the busiest intersections in Delhi, but perhaps in the country. It was the meeting point of the north–south traffic corridor with the east–west corridor, with thousands of vehicles plying across it every minute. Since Rajeev Goswami was fighting for his life in the nearby Safdarjung Hospital, the agitating students of Delhi decided to make the AIIMS crossing the base of their revolt against the government. They squatted at the intersection in the thousands, blocking traffic and bringing the city to a near halt. The blockade was, in media circles, compared to the Tiananmen Square protests of mid-1989 in Beijing, the memories of which were fresh in everyone's mind.

The formidable student movement against job reservations and the creation of OBCs witnessed 200 self-immolation attempts. Sadly, sixty-two students succumbed to their burns. Almost every opposition party supported the agitation, some more overtly than others, but they never stated so in explicit terms. To support the agitation overtly meant opposing reservations approved for OBCs, which in turn would have meant alienating 51 per cent of the voters. Therefore, the opposition leaders restricted themselves to criticizing police action and sympathizing with the families of those students who had immolated themselves.

A few days later, while controlling unlawful crowds near INA market (again in south district), I ordered my boys to resort to lathi charge and tear-gas the mob if the situation called for it. The mob refused to disperse and resorted to large-scale arson and vandalism. They were about to burn down a post office, and we had to open fire at the crowd, during which one rioter was injured. These proceedings were caught on camera by *Newstrack*—a popular video magazine during those days. *Newstrack*'s cameras captured four policemen carrying an injured person away from the scene in a rather unacceptable manner by holding him by his arms and legs while his torso hung loose. The programme in its report highlighted how the four cops hadn't deemed it necessary to use a stretcher, which made it a revolting sight to watch. The fact of the matter was that it was expedient to remove the injured at the soonest for prompt medical attention. The video was viewed widely and the police in my district came under huge criticism. A PIL was filed against the south district police in the Delhi High Court. The advocates who filed the PIL owed allegiance to a national political party opposed to the Janata Dal government in power.

The best lawyers in the country were to appear against us in the PIL hearings. We were in dire need of a good lawyer to present our side of the story. To our dismay, not a single advocate worth his salt was prepared to take up our case. The case had become too sensational and political, with public opinion riding high against us. We requested one lawyer after another to come on board and argue on our behalf, but none was ready to accept our brief. We were losing heart and getting desperate when someone suggested the name of Bawa Gurcharan Singh. Our inquiries revealed that he was an experienced and competent advocate who was apolitical and kept a low profile but was sincere and effective.

I decided to meet Gurcharan Singh and went to his residential office in Model Town along with some of my officers. He was our last chance. When we entered his office, a modest workplace, one look at the middle-aged unassuming man convinced me that we had come to the right place. He greeted us politely and lent us a sympathetic ear as we shared the details of our case with him and requested him to defend us. After hearing us out, he consented to appear for us on one condition. We had to first convince him that the firing by the police at INA market had indeed been necessary.

Several briefings followed after this first meeting wherein I, along with my officers, struggled to justify our actions with evidence, legal provisions and police rules. The lawyer grilled us for hours, often making us feel frustrated and dejected. We felt guilty even without a trial. But, like any competent lawyer, he did his due diligence to convince himself that he was defending a police action that was necessary and justified. Finally, he informed us he was ready to represent us in court.

The hearings in the PIL went on for months. On the days of important hearings, I would make it a point to be present in the court. To see Gurcharan Singh take on the advocates appearing against us and give them a run for their money was to witness court craft at its very best. Whenever I couldn't attend court, Gurcharan Singh would drive down to my office after the hearings and brief me on the proceedings of the day. When I was unavailable, he would call me to keep me updated. Over a period of time, despite the years between us, Gurcharan Singh and I forged a close bond of friendship and mutual respect.

After protracted hearings the court pronounced its verdict. In its final order, the Delhi High Court, far from indicting us, appreciated the police action and observed that had it not been for the police firing, there would have been mayhem in INA market. It was a historic verdict in our favour. What began as an anti-police tirade ended up becoming a feather in our cap. Relief and joy were writ large on the faces of the south district police officers.

Gurcharan Singh drove down to my office soon after the verdict was delivered. I received him outside my office, hugged him and thanked him profusely for what he had achieved on our behalf. If not for his dedication, hard work and rare calibre, this day would have eluded us. The dignified lawyer was happy but humble as we lavished him with praise and appreciation for his unwavering support at a time when the rest of his brethren had deserted us. He said, 'You people did your job well and I tried to do mine as well as I could.'

In the months that followed, as it usually happens, both of us became preoccupied with our respective worlds. Contact between us gradually diminished, until the phone by my bedside rang late one night.

On 6 June 1991, less than a year since we had first met, I was jolted awake by the shrill ringing of the telephone. A relative of Gurcharan Singh was on the line, and he said he had bad news for me. His voice quivered as he spoke. He told me that earlier that evening my friend had been shot dead by three unknown assailants. I couldn't believe what I heard. What, who, how, why were some of the questions I needed the answers to. The grief-stricken caller hung up. I was left in a state of shock by the suddenness of it all.

It had been barely a year since I had got to know this extraordinary lawyer. In that brief period of time, he had worked diligently for us, saved our prestige and procured a landmark judgment in our favour. All this he had achieved in the face of hostile public opinion. He had left an indelible impression on me with his legal acumen, humility and friendship. It was not easy to come to terms with what had just happened.

* * *

Days later, I learnt of the sequence of events that had led to the tragic killing of Gurcharan Singh. The advocate was representing the state against Brij Mohan Sharma, a notorious gangster who operated in Uttar Pradesh and Delhi, in a case of murder. Gurcharan Singh, as always, was brilliant in his arguments against the accused. Brij Mohan realized that if the lawyer continued with his prosecution, his conviction was certain. He shared his fears with his friend Manjeet Singh, another inveterate criminal from Agra. Together, after a court hearing, they threatened the lawyer with dire consequences if he did not give up the case. Gurcharan Singh told them, 'If I were to back off from a case because of threats from goons like you, I better leave practising law.' The goons then called up his wife and warned her that if her husband did not relent he would be done away with. When she brought the conversation to her husband's attention, he brushed her off summarily. The accused, finding the lawyer unyielding, decided to silence him once and for all.

On that fateful evening, at about 8.45 p.m., Gurcharan Singh was at his residential office with his associate Krishna Tyagi. He was dictating a brief to his stenographer, J.S. Oberoi, for a client, who was also present. That was when he spotted a young boy peeping into his office through the glass door. He waved the boy in.

The youngster entered Gurcharan Singh's chamber but with him two other men also sneaked in. Gurcharan Singh, engrossed in a file, raised his head to greet the boy but was startled to see the two men beside him. He recognized them immediately, as they were the ones who had threatened him in court. Before he could react, both of them pulled out their revolvers and shot him at point-blank range, killing him on the spot.

In the melee that followed, Krishna Tyagi slipped out of the room to call the police. The cops reached the spot, investigated the case and identified the killers as Brij Mohan Sharma, Manjeet Singh and Gerard Innis aka Jerry. Manjeet and Jerry were soon arrested by the Delhi Police. Brij Mohan, however, absconded, formed another gang and continued to commit heinous crimes, particularly kidnappings for ransom, mainly in UP.

On 30 July 1991, not even two months after murdering Bawa Gurcharan Singh, Brij Mohan and three of his gang members, kidnapped a property dealer from Jhansi. They asked his family to deliver the ransom money on 5 August at a hotel in Mathura, where the Jhansi Police led by Shailendra Sagar, SSP, had an encounter with the kidnappers. Brij Mohan Sharma was killed in the exchange of fire and the kidnapped person was rescued. Eight years later, on 14 May 1999, the sessions court in Delhi convicted Manjeet Singh and sentenced him to life imprisonment, while Jerry was acquitted.

* * *

And now, almost nineteen years later, stood before me Manjeet Singh, claiming he was the main killer of my beloved friend.

I stared at Manjeet as he humbly confessed to his crime before me. I wondered if he understood the full import of the ghastly crime he had been a party to. How pulling the trigger of his gun had taken away a precious life, caused acute grief to a family and left a void in the lives of all those who knew Gurcharan Singh.

I asked him in all earnestness, 'Why did you kill such a nice man?'

'For the sake of my friendship with Brij Mohan,' was his cold reply.

The details of the murder that he shared with me were, more or less, known to me. I heard Manjeet out and looked at him, my gaze filled with rage and bitterness. How could he have done it? How did he have the gumption to stand before me and admit that it was he who had pulled the trigger to shoot my defenceless friend? I was overcome by a strong desire to get up and do something to him. But Manjeet continued to look into my eyes with meekness and a certain earnestness that was disarming. I couldn't bring myself to even shout at him. I asked him to leave and returned to my office, emotionally drained.

* * *

In the days that followed, I was engrossed in my work at the prison. Every time I managed a visit to jail number two, I would spot Manjeet going about his work silently and devotedly. On a couple of occasions, his request for the grant of parole was presented before me. His case was always recommended by his jail superintendent on account of his good behaviour and his past record of returning from paroles on time and without any complaints during his leave of absence.

In the nineteen years he had served thus far, he had gone on parole several times. Unlike other jail convicts, not once had he jumped parole or delayed his return to jail. His behaviour since the day he had arrived at Tihar had been exemplary and the staff and convicts had great regard for him.

Under Indian law, people who are sentenced to life imprisonment become eligible for a review of their sentence after fourteen years. The remaining part of their sentence can be waived or commuted by the Sentence Review Board, which is appointed by the Government of Delhi. I learnt that Manjeet's case had come up before the board five times and had been repeatedly rejected. The board was meeting next on 20 April 2011. My presence, as the head of Tihar Prisons, was required at the meeting, as the ex officio member secretary.

It had been close to five months since I had taken over as the director general of prisons. I had learnt a lot about the punishment, reformation and rehabilitation of convicts during this time. From being a hardened cop, whose mission in life was to send offenders behind bars, I had begun to see things 'from the other side' and in a very different light. I had realized that there was much more to dealing with criminals than sending them to jail. We had to reform them and give them another chance at an honest life. They were, after all, human beings, many of whom had committed crimes under circumstances that had forced them to take the law into their own hands. If during their imprisonment they showed signs of repentance, remorse and the desire to be reformed, they deserved rehabilitation and integration with mainstream society.

Once again, I called upon the jail superintendent and his support staff and asked them to share their thoughts on the commutation of Manjeet's sentence. They told me that they were all of the opinion that the remaining part of Manjeet's sentence should be commuted. But they were sceptical of a favourable verdict from the Sentence Review Board, as his case had been rejected five times.

On 20 April 2011, Sheila Dikshit, the then chief minister (CM) of Delhi, chaired a meeting of the Sentence Review Board. Cases of convicts serving life sentences in Tihar Prisons were to be considered for commutation. Other members of the board included the principal home secretary, the judicial secretary, the district and sessions judge, the chief probation officer, the joint commissioner of police of crime, and sundry other officials. After the board reviewed two or three other cases, Manjeet's matter came up for discussion. As on the five earlier occasions, when his case had been considered and rejected, once again the entire board was of the opinion that he deserved no mercy. After all, he had killed an eminent advocate in cold blood, only because he (the advocate) was doing his duty as a special prosecutor. The most vocal amongst the board members were the judicial secretary and the sessions judge, who considered themselves to be members of the same fraternity as the deceased victim. The board was unanimously firm that Manjeet should breathe his last within the confines of Tihar. For a ruthless criminal like him, life sentence meant life sentence, period.

Finally, having heard everyone else, the chief minister turned to me for my view. I informed the board that if anyone in the room should oppose the commutation of Manjeet's life sentence tooth and nail, it should be me. I gave the CM and the others present the background of my association with Gurcharan Singh, how he had come to our rescue when all seemed lost and how beholden I was to him till date. Yet, ironically, it was I who was pleading for mercy for my saviour's killer.

I went on to say that I had observed Manjeet Singh from close quarters. I had always found him to be disciplined and well behaved. Most importantly, I felt he was at peace with himself and the world. During the nineteen years that he had spent in prison, there had been no complaints against him. With his consistent record of good behaviour he had won the confidence of the jail staff, so much so that he had begun to assist them in running the jail. He had educated himself in prison and had acquired a graduate degree, following which he was teaching others. He had gone out on parole and furloughs umpteen times and had always returned on schedule with no complaints from anyone. Additionally, I argued, Manjeet had undergone nineteen years of rigorous imprisonment for his crime and no useful purpose would be served by keeping him in custody. I went on to say that I was convinced that he was fully reformed and deserved a chance to live his life with his family, like a normal citizen.

I do not consider myself an orator and public speaking has never been my strong suit. But that afternoon, pleading the case of a convicted murderer before the Sentence Review Board, I felt as though someone else was speaking in my voice. Perhaps it was Gurcharan Singh himself who had pardoned his killer and wished to set him free.

I am not sure whether every member of the review board agreed with me, but each one of them heard me out patiently. After my brief submission, the CM said, 'We have heard a completely new perspective concerning the convict. If the director general of prisons himself feels that the convict is reformed, we should go by his judgment. The convict should be shown mercy and his remaining sentence should be commuted.'

No one dissented once the CM had given her verdict. It gave me happiness to know that my argument would set a man doomed to die within the confines of jail free.

The government order commuting Manjeet's sentence arrived at the jail a few days later. One morning, the superintendent of jail number two informed me that Manjeet had requested a meeting with me before his release the following day. I agreed to meet him one last time.

The two of us met in the superintendent's office the following day. He stood wearing his own clothes, looking rather dapper. Even though it was only a regular blue shirt and a pair of dark blue trousers, they sat well on his broad muscular frame, and he looked like an ageing Hollywood actor ready to give a shot before the camera. It appeared as though he had long prepared for this day. He looked at me with hands folded in supplication and tears in his eyes.

Manjeet said that after his case had been rejected five times, he had lost hope of ever being free. The prospect of

his returning home and leading a respectable life with his
family had gradually faded away. He was resigned to his fate
of spending his life in captivity. But somehow, when he met
me for the first time in the jail garden and spoke to me, his
hope for freedom had been rekindled. Even though he had
seen the rage seething in my eyes following his confession,
he had also sensed forgiveness and compassion. The jail staff
had, from time to time, reassured him that if anyone could
grant him freedom, it would be me.

I too was overwhelmed with emotion. I told him that he
had reformed himself and deserved his freedom. I wished the
best for him and asked him to keep in touch. He folded his
hands again and looked at me as tears of gratitude welled up
in his eyes. As he was leaving, I stood up to see him off. The
prison doors would soon close for the last time on him, setting
him free forever. He was about to make a new beginning in
his life. He turned around and hesitated. Then he hugged me
and walked through the huge steel doors of the jail. He had
spent nineteen years, six months and ten days in prison.

When, at the end of a long police operation—full of
near catches and close misses, sudden rushes of adrenaline
and crushing feelings of disappointment—a dreaded
criminal is arrested, a police officer experiences a feeling of
overwhelming catharsis and euphoria. This feeling is hard
to describe. It is a special feeling that perhaps no other
profession can offer. I have been fortunate to experience this
on a few dozen occasions. But, helping Manjeet Singh walk
free gave me a different kind of high, and that too is difficult
to describe. It was an 'operation' of a different kind that gave,

with its success, a sense of satisfaction not experienced after apprehending big-time criminals.

It has been seven years since Manjeet Singh walked free. To this day, I receive an occasional phone call or a letter from him. Manjeet Singh, the killer of Bawa Gurcharan Singh, is now a full-time farmer, living in his village in Agra district—far from the madding crowd of crime and criminals.

5

Story of Their Assassins

Atal Bihari Vajpayee, one of the most venerated leaders of the Bharatiya Janata Party (BJP), became the tenth prime minister of India in 1996. However, his first term was destined to last a mere thirteen days. Subsequently, in May 1998, he was instrumental in forming a National Democratic Alliance (NDA) by bringing together several regional parties that supported the BJP from outside. The NDA fought the general elections the same year and Vajpayee returned as prime minister. But, yet again, within a year, the government collapsed when an ally based in Tamil Nadu withdrew its support. Nonetheless, with the support of a few more regional parties, the NDA proceeded to win the 1999 elections with a comfortable majority and finally completed its term, which ended in 2004. Vajpayee thus became the first prime minister from outside the Indian National Congress to serve a full five-year term.

The NDA government under Vajpayee witnessed many crises after it came to power on 13 October 1999. Within a little over two months, on 24 December 1999, Indian Airlines

flight IC 814 from Kathmandu to New Delhi was hijacked
by five Al-Qaeda-linked terrorists and flown to Kandahar
in Taliban-ruled Afghanistan. The hijackers demanded the
release of dangerous terrorists as ransom. Terror masterminds
such as Maulana Masood Azhar, Omar Saeed Sheikh and
Mushtaq Ahmed Zargar, all held in Indian prisons, were
named. The week-long stand-off between the hijackers and
the Government of India concluded on the last day of the
millennium when the government wilted under media and
public pressure and acquiesced to the hijackers' demands.
The then external affairs minister, Jaswant Singh, rather
shamefacedly, flew to Kandahar with the three terrorists and
handed them over to the hijackers. The IC 814 passengers
were released and were flown home on 31 December 1999.
In this terror episode there was one tragic fatality. Rupin
Katyal, a twenty-five-year-old honeymooner, succumbed
to injuries inflicted on him by the hijackers at the Amritsar
airport, where the plane had stopped for refuelling.

A year later, on 22 December 2000, the Red Fort in
Delhi, a symbol of India's pluralism and unity, was attacked
by the terror group LeT, leaving three soldiers and a civilian
dead. More than a terror attack on an iconic monument, it
was a serious portent of bigger things to come, including
the attack on the Indian Parliament on 13 December 2001,
which brought India and Pakistan to the brink of war.

But seven months before the attack on the Parliament,
in March 2001, a crisis hit the Vajpayee government that
severely embarrassed it. Tehelka (which means 'sensation'
in Hindi) was a website started by two intrepid journalists,
namely, Tarun Tejpal and Aniruddha Bahal, in 2000. On

14 March 2001, videos of its first major sting investigation, called 'Operation West End', were broadcast on prime-time television, showing the then BJP president, senior army officers and NDA members accepting bribes from journalists posing as agents and businessmen. The president of the BJP had to resign and subsequently, so did the then defence minister. These events left the BJP red-faced and its alliance on the brink of implosion.

Furthermore, Operation West End and its aftermath prompted Pakistan's spy agency, the ISI, to contrive a diabolical plan to destabilize India. The ISI was closely monitoring the situation in India and reasoned that if Tejpal and Bahal, the co-authors of Operation West End, were to be assassinated, the blame would fall on the ruling party. Every finger would point to the BJP for the murder of the two journalists who had exposed their party president. In the wake of the raging controversy that would follow, alongside negative public opinion, the tenuous majority that the NDA had in the Parliament would be breached and the NDA government would once again fall. India would be plunged into political instability. Characteristically, only the ISI could have hatched such an insidious conspiracy against India.

But, who would carry out the job for the ISI? Who would pull the trigger on Tejpal and Bahal? ISI's experience had taught it that using local criminal dons equipped with trained manpower, local knowledge, weaponry and so on was the best bet. For instance, the ISI had put the leading lights of the Mumbai and Gujarat underworlds to good use to carry out serial blasts in Mumbai in 1993. The terror attack had taken nearly three hundred lives and damaged properties worth millions. However, leading mafia dons, namely, Dawood Ibrahim, Tiger Memon, Mohammad Dossa, Abu Salem and Abdul Lateef—the main architects of the serial blasts—were either in hiding in Pakistan or behind bars. The ISI therefore had to look for someone else, someone equally resourceful and capable, but not yet on the radar of the Indian authorities.

The ISI's 'talent scouts' looked eastwards in India and zeroed in on a crime supremo—a monster par excellence—from Bihar who was capable, still at large and fairly active. Not only that, he was a serving member of Parliament (MP). His name: Mohammad Shahabuddin (MS).

MS is a criminal-turned-politician whose equal would be difficult to find in the annals of crime. Yes, you may find offenders with darker criminal involvements, criminals who are far more cruel and devious; but, in my nearly four-decade-long police career, I haven't heard of anyone who alongside his career in crime has been as successful in politics as MS. He had served as a member of Bihar's legislative assembly for two terms in the 1990s and as an MP for four consecutive terms. His political career thrived until the long arm of the law finally caught up with him.

Born on 10 May 1967 in Partapur village in the Siwan district of Bihar, MS entered the world of crime in 1986 at the age of nineteen. Thereafter, he was involved in several cases of murder, attempts to murder and other grave crimes. An example of one such gruesome crime is the case in which he was accused of killing three brothers by giving them an acid bath. The police declared him a habitual offender and opened his history sheet.

Notwithstanding his criminal record, he entered politics and contested the Bihar assembly elections in 1990 and won. He was elected again as a member of the legislative assembly (MLA) in 1995. His political stature grew when he was given a ticket by Rashtriya Janata Dal (RJD) president, Lalu Prasad Yadav, in the parliamentary elections of 1996. Given his reign of terror in Siwan—his home constituency—he won the elections comfortably and became an MP. Riding the wave of his political success, he became a law unto himself in Siwan and often came into confrontation with the local police and government officials. He assaulted policemen with impunity and is known to have fired at them on several occasions.

In March 2001, Sanjiv Kumar, a police officer who had gone to serve a warrant of arrest to MS's party worker, Manoj Kumar Pappu, was slapped by the don. MS's men brutally beat up several policemen accompanying Sanjiv Kumar. The cops had to beat a hasty retreat but soon regrouped. Reinforcements were called, some even from the neighbouring state of Uttar Pradesh. The Siwan police, with an adequate force at their command, raided MS's fortress-like house. In the extensive armed exchange that followed, two policemen and eight of MS's men were killed. Three AK-47s and other automatic weapons were found near the dead bodies of MS's men. MS, along with those of his men still alive, escaped, setting fire to three police jeeps and firing continuously to cover their movement. Neither MS nor Manoj Kumar could be arrested. After this episode, several more cases were filed against MS, but he always absconded.

It was precisely at this time, when MS was on the run, that the ISI decided to contact him and task him with the

killing of the Tehelka duo. MS had been in touch with
Kashmiri separatists and ISI agents for some time, as was
publicly disclosed in a press conference by the then director
general of police (DGP), Bihar. Soon after the DGP made this
announcement, he was posted to an innocuous assignment;
such was MS's political clout.

An ISI agent based in Bangladesh, code-named Jain Saheb,
was in touch with a stooge in Nepal: Salim Mian Ansari.
Ansari was a prominent mafia leader and a former minister
of Nepal. He belonged to the Communist Party of Nepal
(Unified Marxist–Leninist). Two conspiratorial meetings
were held at Salim Mian's Nepal residence sometime around
January–February 2001. MS and Jain Saheb were invited.
MS, aware of what the meeting was about, had taken a
sharpshooter, Bhupender Tyagi, with him. Tyagi hailed from
Uttar Pradesh. MS thought he would be an ideal handyman
to accompany him.

Before proceeding with the story, it would be pertinent
to give a brief background on Tyagi. He was a native of
Kisola village in the Bulandshahr district of Uttar Pradesh.
His father was a cloth merchant and ran a reasonably
successful business. A local goon wanted to extort 'rangdari
tax' (protection money) from the cloth merchant, which he
refused to pay. In the presence of Tyagi, the goon began to
beat his father black and blue for refusing to pay him. An
enraged Tyagi, then aged only eighteen, picked up a metal
ruler—used to measure cloth—and hit the goon on his head,
splitting his skull into two. The goon collapsed and died on
the spot. Fearing arrest, Tyagi ran away from home. He had
little money or personal belongings. He wandered from one

place to another, spending nights at relatives' homes, but soon realized no one was going to give him shelter on a long-term basis. It was at this stage that he ran into a few local criminals and began to work with them, soon realizing he had a flair for crime. He saw a bright future for himself in the underworld.

A friend he ran into during this period had just been released from Ambala Central Jail. The friend told Tyagi that a certain jail employee had been particularly nasty to him and had abused him sexually. Tyagi was enraged and decided to teach the jailor a lesson. He killed the jailor with his bare hands as the man was leaving the prison complex one evening after completing his shift.

Tyagi's criminal friends had begun to spread word of his derring-do in the nether world of crime. His next assignment came from the rival of a sugar mill owner, again in Ambala. The rival wanted the mill owner to be eliminated and was prepared to pay Rs 3 lakh for the job. Tyagi did not bat an eyelid and killed the mill owner with a borrowed weapon. With the money he received, he bought two Chinese-made pistols and thereafter didn't need to look elsewhere for weapons.

It wasn't long before Tyagi decided to form his own gang. He didn't trust the sort of criminals he had met thus far. He began to motivate his first cousins, some of whom were jobless and wished to make a career in crime. At this time, he met one Harey Ram Sant, a dreaded criminal from Gopalganj, Bihar, who had come to visit relatives in the Bulandshahr district. Both Tyagi and Sant hit it off well and decided to work together. But destiny had willed otherwise, at least in the short term.

The Uttar Pradesh Police caught up with Tyagi in 1995. He was arrested and sent to Roorkee Jail. Desperate, he sent word to Sant to help him escape. Towards the end of 1997, with Sant's help, Tyagi fled from police custody while he was being escorted back to Muzaffarnagar Jail from the Roorkee court. He ran straight to Gopalganj where he met Sant, who welcomed him into his gang with open arms. Upon realizing Tyagi was meant for bigger things in the world of crime, Sant introduced him to one Mukul Rai, a local gangster with political links. Rai in turn took Tyagi to Suraj Bhan, a notorious criminal-turned-politician of Bihar. Bhan, then an MLA, sheltered him in Mokama at his own residence. Tyagi was given a 9 mm pistol and trained in the handling of an AK-47 along with other automatic and semi-automatic weapons. Thereafter, he committed over two dozen murders as a hired assassin of Bhan and any businessmen willing to pay him to settle scores with their rivals. One of these murders was the sensational elimination of Tun Tun Singh, an extortionist businessman based in Motihari, Bihar.

Soon, Bhan realized Tyagi was more than a handful, and in 1998, he asked Mukul Rai to introduce Tyagi to an even bigger crime lord. He was taken to Mohammad Shahabuddin. Tyagi was just the sort of gang member MS was looking for—desperate, unscrupulous and daring. Tyagi committed several sensational crimes at MS's behest, including the infamous adhivakta (advocate) murder case of 2000 in which Tyagi killed Raghubir Sharan, an advocate and a witness in a case against MS's aide Manoj Kumar aka Pappu. He did not hesitate to kill Sharan's wife and their ten-year-old son, who were witnesses to Sharan's cold-blooded murder.

Some months later, on 15 January 2001, Tyagi went on to commit the Roshera 'narsanhar' (massacre) in which seven people were killed and nineteen seriously injured, although the target was only one person, namely, Murari, a small-time criminal who had the gumption to elope with the sister of one of Tyagi's gang members.

Tyagi's march in the criminal world continued relentlessly with umpteen bank robberies, kidnappings for ransom, hired killings and so on. He would kill for money with no remorse, spreading a reign of terror in north Bihar.

* * *

Having agreed to carry out the kill for the ISI, MS dispatched Tyagi to Delhi with the promise that weapons would be delivered to him there once his team and he were ready for the hit. Tyagi arrived in Delhi and put together a small team of local goons without any criminal records. The Delhi Police had no clue about their criminal propensities. Tyagi, along with his rookie gang members, carried out a recce of the journalists' residences and their office. Tyagi was in regular touch with his ISI handlers, who were based in Kathmandu. Fortunately, a telephone call that he made to a number in Nepal in connection with this conspiracy was intercepted by one of the central intelligence agencies of the Government of India. The intercept was shared with the Special Cell of Delhi Police, which promptly began to monitor all numbers that were being called from the Nepal number and those calling it.

* * *

It was early May 2001. I was posted as a joint director in the Economic Offences Wing of the CBI, having already completed nearly eight years of my deputation in the organization. I had maintained close links with my parent force—the Delhi Police—particularly with its counterterrorism wing, the Special Cell. My team in the CBI and officers from the cell had carried out several successful operations jointly. Consequently, in true esprit de corps, we freely shared details of our work with one another and sought mutual help as and when necessary. I was thus privy to the developments in the operation to save the Tehelka duo and arrest their assassins before they struck.

The cell was racing against time and two precious lives were at stake, as was the fate of the NDA government. Our hopes for a breakthrough were pinned solely on the chatter on nearly twenty mobiles we were secretly listening in to. But all we heard were conversations in chaste Haryanvi about property deals, plans to grab land on the outskirts of Delhi, unauthorized constructions and so on. It was clear they were toughs who were in the business of grabbing land, forcible evictions, etc. The waiting game was nerve-racking. The high-stakes operation was making no progress and waiting any longer for something to give made no sense.

Meanwhile, the dilemma before us was whether or not to caution the Tehelka honchos. If we informed them, it was unlikely they would keep the news to themselves. With little trust in the Delhi Police, they would run to the high and mighty in the Central government to provide them with special security. Also, they would go to town with the information about the impending threat to their lives, which would certainly make sensational headlines. Therefore, without taking the journalists into confidence, we quietly cast a protective ring around them, lest the assassins strike.

As waiting any longer was foolhardy, it was decided to round up all those who were under surveillance. The fact that the initial information had come from a central intelligence agency made expediency that much more imperative. But one premature move, one slip-up and the game could be over. Picking the goons up in ones and twos could have resulted in the rest escaping and jeopardizing our operation to nip the conspiracy in the bud. We wanted to lay our hands, in one clean swoop, on as many of them as possible, and sooner rather than later.

Finally, we heard in one of the intercepts that most of the goons were to meet near Bhalswa dairy in north-west Delhi. A trap was laid and we lay in wait.

On 5 May 2001 a Tata Safari with licence plate number DL 8CF 5xx5 was spotted near the rendezvous point off the Delhi–Karnal highway. Six goons, later identified as Anil Kumar Shehrawat, Raj Kumar, Rakesh, Dinesh Kumar, Omvir and Bhupender Tyagi aka Modi were nabbed from the vehicle. An AK-47 rifle with two magazines and 200 rounds of ammunition, one pistol with two magazines and fifty rounds of ammunition and fake Indian currency worth Rs 25,000 were recovered. Most importantly, layout plans of the residences of Tejpal and Bahal and their office at D1 Swami Nagar in Delhi were also found. The following day, one more AK-47 rifle with two magazines, 100 rounds of ammunition and one pistol with ammunition were recovered from the house of Anil Kumar Sehrawat.

With the arrest of Tyagi, whose curriculum vitae in the criminal world has been discussed earlier, and his five associates, the attempted assassination of Tejpal and Bahal was foiled. A case of criminal conspiracy to commit murder was registered at the police station in Lodhi Colony against the arrested accused and MS, who was absconding.

* * *

It was somewhere around this time that I went to my hometown Patna to visit my parents. When returning to Delhi, I was sitting in the lounge at Patna airport, waiting for my flight. As I sat browsing through newspapers, I heard a commotion and looked around. Lo and behold, I saw MS walking into the lounge nonchalantly. An aide, who was carrying his briefcase, accompanied him. A member of the airline staff was escorting the two and told them he would come to inform them once boarding commenced. They slumped into a sofa, relaxed and comfortable.

I had recognized MS instantly as he had walked in. His unmistakable tall frame, neatly trimmed moustache and piercing gaze were enough for me to identify him. But since this was the first time I was seeing him in the flesh, I wanted to be absolutely sure that it was indeed him. Here I was, face-to-face with one of the most dreaded criminals of the time, wanted in several cases, one of which I was intimately privy to. I had to do something fairly quickly as within minutes both he and I would be flying off, not necessarily to the same destination. I was fidgety and restless while he was carefree and unconcerned. He was obviously not aware that a CBI officer had spotted him. Not that it would have mattered. After all, he was an MP and someone police officers usually kept away from. I stepped outside the lounge to speak to Neelu Babu, a Special Branch officer of the Bihar Police deployed at the airport, who had come to see me off.

'Who is the man who just walked into the lounge?' I enquired.

'Sir, he is the same person you think he is,' replied Neelu.

By now I could feel the adrenaline rush. The only other flight taking off at that time had been announced and passengers had begun boarding. MS and his crony were still sitting coolly in the lounge. That meant he was on the same flight as I was and we were both Delhi-bound.

I asked Neelu if I could use a phone with STD facility. He quickly took me to a booth nearby, installed in an open cabin without any privacy. But I had to alert my counterparts in the Delhi Police Special Cell who were investigating the case MS was wanted in. I called up Rajbir Singh, an ACP in the Special Cell, and informed him that I was taking the Indian Airlines flight to Delhi that day and that he should meet me at the Delhi airport with a small police team. I didn't wish to take MS's name within hearing distance of anyone lest the word leak out. My message to Rajbir was cryptic but clear enough for him to come prepared for some action.

Meanwhile, the flight had been announced, and I proceeded towards security check. MS stayed put, as the airline staffer had not yet turned up to escort him. Fortunately for me, my seat, 7C, was an aisle seat in the first row of economy class. I could easily see what was going on in business class. Sure enough, I saw MS board the aircraft and take seat 1F in the first row of the executive class, while his associate walked into economy and moved towards the rear rows. I could easily see MS from my seat. By now my excitement knew no bounds. A wanted criminal was travelling in the same flight as I was.

Once the aircraft door closed, the airhostess welcomed the passengers aboard the flight going to Delhi via Ranchi. Via Ranchi? Oh my god! That threw cold water on my excitement. I had alerted the Special Cell to be ready for an operation, but what if our quarry disembarked at Ranchi? All through the barely half-hour flight to Ranchi I had ants in my pants, wondering what would happen at Ranchi. Would MS get off or would he continue on to Delhi? The suspense was killing me. What was required of me if he was indeed Delhi-bound? I had to try hard not to give away my anxiety and restlessness to the passengers seated close to me.

Soon the aircraft landed at Ranchi and my fears were put to rest. Neither MS nor his crony disembarked. Once the Ranchi-bound passengers had alighted, I walked towards the rear of the aircraft and saw MS's aide seated in 27E. I decided it was now necessary to inform the Special Cell that it was MS who was travelling with me and was seated in 1F while his associate was in 27E.

I told the airhostess who I was and that I needed to alight and make an urgent official call. She informed me that Delhi-bound passengers were not permitted to disembark. I then told her I needed to see the captain and gave her my CBI visiting card. Within a minute she was back to inform me that the captain wanted to see me in the cockpit immediately.

I told the captain that I had an urgent message to convey to my fellow officers in Delhi and I needed to make a call immediately. Both the captain and I carried mobile phones but mobile telephony had not yet come to Ranchi. He permitted me to disembark and assured me that the flight would wait for me. I quickly got off the aircraft and ran to the terminal building. To my surprise, there was not a soul to be seen there. Ours was the last flight to leave Ranchi, and once the last passengers had left the terminal to board the flight to Delhi, all ground staff deployed at the airport had left.

I ran around the terminal building like a mad man. Thankfully, I noticed a man in uniform with Central Reserve Police Force (CRPF; the Central Industrial Security Force [CISF] had not taken over airport security at Ranchi yet) shoulder tabs. I rushed up to him, introduced myself and said that I needed to make an urgent call. He took me to the CRPF office, which was located within the terminal building. I rang up Rajbir Singh and excitedly informed him that it was MS and an associate of his who were travelling on my flight. I also shared with him their seat numbers.

The standard operating procedure followed by law enforcement agencies when they have to pick up somebody from an aircraft is that the captain is informed beforehand through air traffic control not to commence disembarkation until the agency officers enter the aircraft, locate the person to be picked up and leave with their quarry. I felt satisfied that I had conveyed all the necessary information to the concerned officers. I could now return to the aircraft in peace for the onward journey to Delhi. The stage was set for the smooth apprehension of one of the most dreaded criminals of our time. Or so I thought.

As I emerged from the Ranchi airport terminal building after making the call, I saw the aircraft waiting for me with the boarding stairs still in place. Boarding had been completed and there was not a soul around. An eerie silence prevailed as I ran up the steps and entered the aircraft, panting. I could feel the glares of the passengers already seated whose flight had been delayed because of me. The airhostess, however, greeted me with a smile and whispered to me to proceed to the cockpit.

The captain welcomed me back, saying, 'Sir, you look very anxious. Why don't you calm down and sit with us in the cockpit?'

No better offer could have come to me at that point. My frayed nerves relaxed as I sat on the seat right behind the captain. The airhostess served me a glass of juice. I noticed that the co-pilot was a lady.

The aircraft soon took off and was on its way to Delhi. After the seat belt sign was turned off, the pilots got chatting with me.

The captain asked, 'Sir, can you tell me why you are so exercised?'

There was no reason for me to be secretive after what the captain had done for me. 'Captain, there is a wanted criminal on board.'

'Is he the gentleman sitting in 1F?'

My reply was in the affirmative, but I inquired how he knew.

'I fly this circuit often and know the frequent fliers, particularly the VIPs,' he said with a smile.

The irony of a wanted criminal being a VIP frequent flier was not lost on me.

There was silence for a while.

The co-pilot then said, 'Sir, I had heard so much about CBI officers chasing criminals but for the first time I am seeing it happen right in front of my eyes.' She looked at me in awe.

The flying time between Ranchi and Delhi passed quickly, thanks to the hospitality of the pilots and the cabin staff. Soon the aircraft was approaching Delhi. The captain offered to convey any message that I wanted through air traffic control, once the plane had landed. Alternatively, I could switch on my mobile phone as soon as the aircraft had touched the tarmac. I thanked him for the offer and informed him that all necessary information had already been conveyed.

The aircraft landed smoothly at Delhi and began to taxi to its designated spot. I called up Rajbir, but uncharacteristically, there was no response even as his mobile and landline phones rang incessantly. I then called up his deputy, Inspector Mohan Chand Sharma, but even he didn't respond. This was a strange and unacceptable turn of events.

Meanwhile, the aircraft had finished taxiing and had come to a stop. I waited anxiously for the Special Cell boys to rush in and nab MS and his aide. But there was no one in sight. Both the captain and co-pilot looked at me quizzically and asked my permission to let the passengers disembark. I must have looked like a fool after the larger-than-life picture I had painted of a CBI sleuth in action through the flight. Embarrassed, I called Rajbir one last time from my mobile, but there was again no response. I then called Mohan Sharma.

But there was no response from him either. Never before had Rajbir or his deputy not answered a call from me or not called me back immediately.

I knew something was amiss but could not figure out what. I had no option but to tell the captain to allow the passengers to disembark. I was permitted to leave with the business class passengers in the first bus. There, standing almost next to me, was MS. He obviously did not know of me or recognize me. On reaching the terminal building, he calmly left, right in front of my eyes. My last hope of the Special Cell picking him up from the arrival area had vanished into thin air.

* * *

After collecting my check-in baggage I exited the terminal and drove straight to the Special Cell office. I was furious at being let down, and that too with such brazenness. I stormed into Rajbir's office and saw him sitting with Mohan Sharma. I shouted at them for their strange behaviour and demanded an explanation. They were not my subordinates as I was in the CBI and they in the Delhi Police. But, we had worked together as a team on several occasions and I felt I had the moral right to question them. In any case, I was their senior in police hierarchy by many ranks. Rajbir calmed me down after I had given full vent to my fury. He then gave me his side of the story.

On receiving the information about MS from me, Rajbir had shared it with his immediate superiors who had thought it prudent to get the approval of their political

bosses, particularly because MS was an MP. The permission
to apprehend him had been denied. The two officers were
also under instructions from their immediate superiors to
distance themselves from me for a while. No wonder they
hadn't answered any of my calls.

I was later to learn that some kind of political initiative was
afoot to forge an alliance between MS and other politicians in
Bihar to derail the ruling party there. It did not matter that
MS was wanted in a serious case of conspiracy to derail the
very same government that was denying permission for his
arrest. It also did not matter that MS was regularly in touch
with the ISI and Kashmiri militants.

Thus came to a rather farcical end my effort to get one
of the most dreaded criminals in India arrested after a chance
encounter with him at an airport lounge. Even subsequently,
he was not arrested by the Delhi Police as a co-conspirator in
the case of the attempted assassination of Tejpal and Bahal.
His name was, however, mentioned in the charge sheet of
the case in 'khana (column) number 2' as an accused against
whom sufficient evidence had not come on record.

* * *

Tyagi, in the interim, was under trial with his associates in
the Tarun Tejpal–Aniruddha Bahal assassination attempt
case in the Tees Hazari court. He was often taken by the
Uttar Pradesh Police to the Roorkee, Bulandshahr and
Haridwar courts for cases that were pending trial there. As
the days went by the limelight on Tyagi faded. He was
lodged in Tihar Jail and occasionally taken to courts in and

outside Delhi, escorted by a police guard whose strength kept declining progressively. Tyagi knew it was time for him to flee.

Those who have driven on highways in India are familiar with built-up areas coming up ever so frequently, creeping up to the road within sniffing distance of the busy traffic. Wayside dhabas—eateries popular for their fresh food served steaming hot—petrol stations, motor workshops and grocery stores dot either side of the road in a haphazard and chaotic manner. Pedestrians hop across the road as if they are on a suicide mission. Often, in larger townships, a bus station, with countless passengers carrying all manner of luggage, adds to the cosmic chaos that is India. Decrepit and ramshackle buses, overloaded with passengers, zoom in and out of the terminals, leaving a trail of dust behind them. Small puddles of putrid water dot the landscape like festering wounds. Yet, bus and railway stations in India, with their hustle and bustle, are living testimonies of the energy and drive of the country.

On 13 September 2003, Head Constable Baburam, Constable Ramchander and Constable Neeraj Kumar of the armed police of Uttar Pradesh stood at one such bus stand in Roorkee, a city in the Haridwar district of Uttarakhand in north India. They had in their custody none other than Tyagi. It had been over two years since he had been arrested by the Special Cell of Delhi Police. He had been moved from Tihar Jail to the Muzaffarnagar district jail in Uttar Pradesh, as he was required to appear before courts in that jurisdiction. He was being taken to the Roshnabad district jail of Haridwar from where he had to be produced before the Roshnabad court the following day.

It was an unusually hot and humid post-monsoon afternoon, typical of the plains of north India. The policemen, lugging their .303 rifles, were perspiring in the oppressive heat, their uniforms drenched with sweat and their alertness dipping by the minute. Their detenue Bhupinder Tyagi was equally agitated and fidgety, but not because of the muggy air. He was waiting, rather impatiently, for his freedom.

At about 4 p.m., a red motorcycle with registration number UP 07C 78X1 drove slowly by the group and stopped a couple of yards away. The two riders got off, approached the policemen and began abusing them. Before the cops could react they were pushed to the ground. Tyagi broke free and ran to the bike as did his rescuers. They hopped on to the motorcycle with Tyagi in the middle and began riding away. One of them saw Constable Neeraj Kumar run after them and opened fire at the policeman. Kumar was hit in the chest and fell down. However, almost as a reflex action, from his prone position Kumar aimed his .303 rifle at them and pulled the trigger. The first and only shot fired by him got the hoodlum sitting at the rear end of the bike. Not surprisingly—given its muzzle velocity and the short range—the bullet went through his body, then Tyagi's and finally pierced through the third gangster who was driving the bike. The motorcycle crashed to the ground with its three riders thrown off in a heap. Constable Neeraj Kumar, injured grievously, lay at a distance writhing in pain. He was rushed to the hospital and fortunately survived. The three gangsters, however, were declared dead on arrival at the hospital.

Thus Tyagi's life came to a bloody end, perhaps a fitting culmination to the trail of terror and killings he had unleashed in the plains of north India.

The law finally caught up with MS in September 2016 when he was arrested on the orders of the Patna High Court. Since the prisons in Bihar had earlier failed to keep MS in custody as he had compromised the jail staff, either through intimidation or by lucre, the Supreme Court, in February 2017, on a request made by the Government of Bihar, ordered that he be transferred to Tihar Jail in Delhi.

MS, reportedly a much mellower person now, is cooling his heels in an isolation ward of Tihar. Quite recently, he petitioned the Supreme Court to be moved to the general ward from his solitary confinement. The court dismissed his petition, asking him to submit his request to the director general of Tihar Prisons. Nothing more has been heard since.

With the sahib (lord) behind bars, in a prison located several hundred kilometres away from his fiefdom and where his writ doesn't run, Siwan sleeps better. Kidnappings, dacoities and murders are on the decline and the law and order situation is much better. But given the vicissitudes of politics and our criminal justice system, only time will tell how long the sahib and his riyasat (state) are kept away from each other.

6

Goan Rhapsody

The mere mention of Goa conjures up a kaleidoscopic picture of the sun, sea, sand, seafood and spice. Blessed with over a hundred kilometres of coastline with beautiful beaches—ideal for sunbathing, water sports, swimming and dolphin-watching—this state in the Konkan region of south-west India is arguably the most popular tourist hub in the country. Air charters full of tourists—mostly low-budget and backpackers—land at Goa's Dabolim airport, disgorging their passengers in this sunny paradise. During the winter months—particularly during Christmas and New Year— Goa is flooded with tourists, both from India and overseas, who flock there to soak in its unique festive air.

Goa, of course, is much more than a popular holiday resort. Besides its beaches and trance parties, it is a place rich in history and culture. The hinterland is lush green and idyllic, dotted with beautiful old-time villas, majestic temples and churches boasting a quaint mix of Portuguese and Indian traditions. Ruled for over 450 years by the Portuguese, it undeniably has the feel of a place distinct from other states in India that were ruled by the British. This coupled with its breathtaking natural beauty makes it stand out as a must-see place for anyone visiting India.

Regrettably, the beauty of this land is also its biggest curse. Not only do people want to visit the place but also own a chunk of it. For instance, almost everybody who is somebody in north India craves to own a second home in Goa to escape the bitter winter cold and suffocating smog of Delhi or its satellite towns. The inevitable result is that Goa is slowly turning into a concrete jungle.

I have been to Goa not only as a vacationer but also in a completely different avatar—as its police chief. To be on holiday in Goa and to serve as its police chief are two antithetical experiences. I wish to write about the latter, to give my readers a sense of what it was like working as a police officer in Goa.

But before I do that, a brief background on Goa's political set-up and its history and on how I found my way to Goa.

After its liberation from Portuguese rule in 1961—fourteen years after the rest of India won its independence from the British—Goa was governed by the federal government as a Union territory (UT) and therefore was a part of the Union territory cadre of the All India Services. Delhi, Pondicherry, Andaman and Nicobar Islands, Lakshadweep, Daman and Diu, Chandigarh, Arunachal Pradesh and Mizoram were the other constituents of the cadre. Goa was granted statehood in 1987 and so were the two north-eastern states of Arunachal Pradesh and Mizoram. The UT cadre was rechristened as the AGMUT (Arunachal,

Goa, Mizoram and Union territories) cadre, to which I was allotted on joining the IPS.

Quite early in my career (1980–82), I served in Arunachal as a superintendent of police of Kameng district with my headquarters at Bomdila. I was later posted to Mizoram in January 2004 as inspector general of police (IGP). Thereafter I moved to Goa as the DGP in November 2005. I lasted for barely eleven months there, during which time I had several encounters with local political leaders that provoked their ire. I wish to share a few snapshots of such interactions as the head of the Goa Police.

Having served in the Delhi Police and the CBI for the major part of my career, serving in Goa felt different and onerous, as the police are directly under the political leadership of the state. Political interference awaits the police at all levels, almost on a daily basis. From recruitment of constables and sub-inspectors to their placement and day-to-day functioning, meddling by politicos is commonplace. Non-compliance of their demands by the police, and perhaps by any public servant, is taken as a personal affront.

November—the month I took over as the DGP—was the beginning of the holiday season in Goa. Very soon, it would be inundated with tourists of all hues. Surely, some extra police deployment to manage traffic and to put in place elaborate law and order arrangements would be required. I decided to take stock of the situation and discuss the special steps planned for Christmas and New Year's Eve. I was advised by my junior officers to visit the Baga and Calangute areas, the most crowded parts of Goa during the peak holiday season.

During one of my visits to these areas, the local MLA came to see me, which I thought was a gracious gesture on his part. But I was in for a surprise. Soon after pleasantries were exchanged, he went on to give me a taste of the kind of experiences that awaited me in Goa.

He said, 'Sir, the first thing you need to do is to transfer out the local officer-in-charge of Calangute police station.'

I was taken aback by the abruptness of his demand. I had taken over only a few days earlier and this was our first interaction. I asked him why he wanted the officer to be transferred. The MLA gave an interesting response to my question.

He complained, 'Sir, your officer is not helping me get the nightclub Cabana closed.'

I then asked him why he wanted the said nightclub to be shut down.

He replied nonchalantly, 'Sir, I have a stake in its rival nightclub, called Vito's [name changed]. Ever since Cabana has come up, there has been a steady decline in the footfall at Vito's.'

I couldn't believe the audacity of the man. In our very first meeting he had the temerity to make such an outlandish demand, and then give a reprehensible reason for it. I gave him a bemused look and thought to myself that the officer-in-charge would stay where he was and the MLA could take a hike. I instinctively knew that the police officer whose transfer was being sought must be a no-nonsense man who could stand up to the crooked politician. Later, when I inquired about the officer in question, I was told, not surprisingly, that he was indeed a fine officer who had done

some outstanding work in the area under his charge. There
was no reason whatsoever for him to be moved.

Before proceeding further, I must explain the power
dynamics at work in Goa.

The Goa Legislative Assembly is a small unicameral
legislature with only forty members. Generally, no political
party emerges as a clear winner in any legislative elections.
Whichever party ends up forming the government does so
with the support of other smaller parties and independent
MLAs. The precarious majority in the house is affected
if even one MLA moves from the ruling coalition to the
opposition. Consequently, the delicate political balance can
often be in jeopardy, so much so that the government may
fall. Therefore, it is not uncommon in Goa for MLAs to
flex their political muscles, if their demands—reasonable or
otherwise—are not met. They may even intimidate the chief
minister with the threat of crossing over to the opposition
and pulling down the government.

Quite expectedly, when his request didn't cut any
ice with me, the MLA made a complaint against me to
the CM. He also covertly threatened the CM, as I came
to know later, saying that he would cross over to the
opposition if his demand to transfer the officer-in-charge
at the Calangute police station was not met. The CM
called me and asked me if the MLA's request could be
considered favourably. I shared with him the real reason
why the MLA wanted the officer transferred and said that
in the interest of police morale, the officer should not be
moved. The CM saw the point I was trying to make and
did not pressure me further.

However, the MLA was not willing to give up that easily. I was not prepared to do his bidding, especially after learning the reason behind his demand. Our battle continued for a couple of months. During this time, I had gone on an official visit to Delhi when I received a frantic call from my deputy inspector general (DIG). He informed me that a high-level delegation of the ruling party from Delhi was visiting Goa to take stock of the political situation. In a meeting with the delegation, the same MLA had complained that the CM did not accede to even minor requests of elected representatives, such as the transfer of an officer-in-charge posted in their constituency. A senior party leader, who was heading the delegation, directed the CM to 'look into' the MLA's request forthwith. My DIG had then been summoned by the CM in my absence and asked to issue orders transferring out the officer-in-charge immediately. The DIG was aware of my views on the subject and called me to find out what he should do. I asked him to hold on until I returned and not to issue any orders.

When I flew back to Goa, I drove straight from the airport to the CM's residence. The CM informed me that even though he was not in favour of transferring the officer, he was under tremendous pressure from his party to get it done. Therefore, I had to find a way out.

'Sir, if the officer must be moved, he should be sent to a police station of his choice,' I said as assertively as I could.

The CM immediately agreed.

I called the officer to my office the next day and explained the situation to him. He told me that he would be happy to move out of Calangute as the local MLA was making life difficult for him. When asked to name a police station of his preference, he said that Verna in south Goa would be his choice. His wife was in the family way and required looking after. As the Verna police station was close to his residence, he would get time to devote to her care.

Orders were issued transferring the officer to Verna. I thought I had resolved the issue in the best way possible, but I was in for another surprise. When the officer reported for duty, the MLA of Verna would not allow him to take charge of the police station as he had been posted to the MLA's constituency without consulting him. After all, which politician would want an upright and honest officer, who would not be at his beck and call, to be posted to his area? This infuriated me. I was prepared to go to the CM to take up the issue. Meanwhile, I learnt that the officer had assumed charge at Verna and all was well. Much later, I was informed that the officer-in-charge had realized that it would be a pointless exercise on his part to again take up cudgels against an egotistical politician. He had called on the MLA from Verna and told him to let him know if he could do anything to serve his constituency better. His ego well massaged, the politician did not create any further trouble for the officer.

* * *

As I was learning the ropes of my new job, I came to know that rave parties were common in Goa, where the sale and consumption of narcotic drugs were widely practised alongside other illegal activities. There existed a close-knit community of drug addicts and peddlers, who were most active during the holiday season. They shared details of the venues and times of such parties with each other openly. They had no fear of law enforcement agencies and brazenly distributed leaflets or pasted notices with the details of these parties. These raves, I also learnt, were generally organized at remote islands and other isolated places, away from the public gaze. I was appalled on hearing of this phenomenon, and particularly by the indifference of the Goa Police towards it. I decided to put an end to this practice and stop the open use of narcotic substances and concomitant illegal activities. I asked my juniors to launch a drive against such parties and put a stop to them. Officers-in-charge of police stations were warned that if news of such a party being held in their jurisdiction reached the police headquarters, they would face unpleasant consequences.

Thereafter, a cat and mouse game began between the cops and the organizers of the raves. As soon as we learnt of a venue where such an event was planned, a police picket was deployed there. The venue would then move elsewhere, but thanks to proper intelligence gathering, we would reach there as well. Gradually, the brazen distribution of leaflets and pasting of notices disappeared. Communication between party organizers and drug addicts was now only by word of mouth. However, with a strong network of informants, we were always a step ahead of them and would appear on the scene unexpectedly. Several drug peddlers were caught with narcotic substances in their possession and booked under the Narcotic Drugs and Psychotropic Substances (NDPS) Act.

The fear of god spread amongst the drug community and there was a lull for some time. No information on rave parties being held was forthcoming. But it would be foolish, I told my officers, to lower our guard. Sure enough, information was received that a rave party was to take place at Canacona Island in the extreme south of Goa, bordering Karnataka. I ordered the deployment of officers at the point from where ferries plied to the island. Anyone approaching the ferry point was asked to show their identification papers. No rave party reveller wanted her personal details to be entered into police records and nor were the organizers prepared for a confrontation with the police. Soon, there was nobody in sight at the ferry point. We had succeeded in pre-empting another big rave party. It was possibly the last attempt by the organizers to host a rave party. Or was it? Goa never fails to surprise anyone, and I was no exception.

Shortly after the Canacona experience, one afternoon an MLA from north Goa walked into my office. We chatted cordially until he dropped a bombshell on me.

He lamented, 'DG sahib, with your clampdown on rave parties, you have ruined the reputation of Goa as a holiday destination. Which tourist will come here if you make it a police state?'

Before I could react he asked me, 'What if I were to hold a rave party in the privacy of my farmhouse? Would you raid it as well?'

It took me some time to respond. All I said was, 'Try it.'

He stormed out of my office in a huff, leaving his cup of tea unfinished.

I could sense that the MLA wished to prove a point and was determined to tie up with rave party organizers—clearly people with deep pockets—and have a get-together at his farm. He would undoubtedly earn a substantial sum of money in the bargain. He was sure the police would think twice before raiding an MLA's property.

We lost no time in finding out where his farm was. Near Ashvem, on the Morjim–Tiracol road, a dirt track veered off the road and led to the politician's farm, which was a good 3 kilometres away from the main road. Our informers were alerted and commanded to immediately inform us if they learnt of any rave party being held in that area. Sure enough, within a week of the MLA's visit to my office, we got news that a drug party would soon be held at his farm. We had details of the date and time. The organizers were sure that with the MLA's involvement, and the fact that the party was to take place on his private farm, the police would not dare to come anywhere near them.

All we did was to deploy a police picket at the point where the dirt track branched off the Morjim–Tiracol road. The instructions given to our men were to stop any vehicle approaching the picket and ask its passengers to show their identification papers or their passports. As the checking commenced, news of police presence spread like wildfire in the rave party community of Goa. Vehicles bringing revellers to the party were seen taking U-turns and fleeing. The party was called off, much to the chagrin of the MLA.

He called me, demanding, 'How can you do this? I will report you to the CM.'

I replied, 'We were nowhere close to your property. All that the police were doing was checking travel documents to detect foreigners staying beyond their visa period.'

That was the last I heard from him.

* * *

In March 2006, I had another bizarre experience. We received specific information from a central intelligence agency about a terrorist who was on his way to Goa from Mumbai by train, with plans of causing Bali-like bombings in crowded nightclubs. Some readers may recall that barely six months earlier, on 1 October 2005, bombs exploded at two sites in southern Bali, Indonesia. The blasts claimed the lives of twenty people and injured over a 100 holidaymakers of different nationalities. A similar bombing was planned in Goa, as per the information, to scare away tourists from India and spread terror amongst the people.

A crack team of Goa Police Crime Branch rushed by road to board the Matsyagandha Express—plying between Mumbai and Ernakulum via Margaon in Goa (the train the terrorist was reportedly travelling in)—at a station before Margaon, 35 kilometres from Panaji, the capital. The terrorist, a man in his thirties, was spotted by our boys in one of the train compartments and kept under watch. Another team awaited his arrival at Margaon. As he stepped out of the train, he was taken into custody and whisked away to a safe house. From his possession were recovered a kilogram of explosive material, two Russian-made hand grenades, electronic detonators and the like. We decided to keep his detention under wraps and make him communicate with his handlers over email. The idea was that when he reported to his bosses that he had reached his destination and all was well with him, they would send more men and weapons. Thus, we hoped, we would catch more terrorists and recover more arms and explosives.

On the afternoon of 12 March, the day after Tariq Ahmed Batlo of LeT was picked up, a group of journalists walked into my office. They began to congratulate me on making the arrest. I was taken aback because we had not made the news public. I feigned ignorance and asked them which terrorist they were talking about. Some of them laughed and one reporter, with a mischievous smile on his face, disclosed that the CM himself had made an announcement to that effect in Margaon, only half an hour earlier. I called up the SP of south Goa based in Margaon and inquired if the CM had made such an announcement. The young officer confirmed that indeed the CM had triumphantly declared the 'good news' to the public. But, I wondered how the CM knew of the arrest, as neither my officers nor I had shared the information with him. I found out later that an armed police constable, who was on guard duty with the terrorist, had informed the CM of the arrest. On further inquiry, it was learnt that the constable hailed from the same constituency as the CM and clearly was more loyal to him than to his police chief.

* * *

As DGP of Goa, I met several local people and made lasting friendships. Most of them were chance encounters, but the relationships forged through them have stood the test of time. In early December 2005, my wife and I were at lunch with one such couple when the lady casually mentioned that in north Goa at Morjim, two Russian men ran a popular drug den, complete with trance music and attractive young ladies in attendance. Planeloads of people came from Delhi, Mumbai and other major cities to have fun at the private getaway, tucked in a remote corner of Morjim. These visitors shelled out huge sums of money as entry fee to the premises and indulged in drug abuse and merrymaking. Incredulous to begin with, I had the tip-off verified and found her information to be accurate.

An operation was planned in secrecy wherein the road leading to the private property of the Russians was blocked and all escape routes sealed. When our team raided the house, they found a rave party in full swing with young men and women high on drugs gyrating to the loud music blaring in the background. Some youngsters were lying on the floor, completely stoned. On a systematic search of the premises, kilograms of various kinds of party drugs were discovered hidden in secret cavities and crevices. The rave party was busted; the music came to an abrupt end; revellers ran helter-skelter only to find cops waiting for them at every corner. The two Russians, who were arrested on drug-related charges, were found to be on tourist visas that had long expired. Yet they were happily overstaying and running an illegal establishment for profit.

When I inquired from my officers which other businesses were being run by foreigners without valid business visas, I was surprised to learn that the number was in the hundreds.

A visitor to Goa can get the best of French, Greek, Italian or any other international cuisine at high-end, fine dining restaurants. Foodies amongst the tourists travel long distances to dine at them. I gradually realized that the owners of such restaurants were all foreigners specializing in those cuisines.

Out of sheer curiosity, we decided to carry out a drive to check their travel documents. To our surprise, not even one of them had the requisite business visa. They were all on tourist visas for six months to coincide with the peak tourist season. During this period they ran these restaurants freely. Quite a few of them were virtually settled in Goa, had bought land and were running flourishing businesses with no one to question them. Such foreigners were now being identified, their papers checked and if found without legal papers, they were being deported.

As the drive progressed, a number of such premises closed down and their foreign owners fled. However, I was to realize much later that I was treading on the toes of powerful local people who would soon get even with me.

Amongst the many victims of the drive was a famous foreigner—a German national, Ingo Grill—who ran the hugely popular Ingo's Saturday Night Bazar in Goa, in partnership with a top politician's wife. Inquiries into his business activities showed that since 2002 he had organized flea markets under the aforesaid brand name at different locations in Goa. He had incorporated an eponymous company with the local registrar of companies and had a letter from the Reserve Bank of India (RBI) addressed to M/s Goa Adventure Company, with a Panaji address, conveying approval in his name for acquiring equity shares as a foreigner.

As inquiries were under way, several people occupying positions of authority asked me why I was taking such a keen interest in Ingo's affairs. When informed that all the foreigners running businesses in Goa were being probed, I was given hints to back off in the case of Ingo. When the inquiries continued unabated, first my juniors—mostly officers from Goa—were intimidated. In their defence they said they were only carrying out orders. It was then my turn to be pressured and to receive veiled threats. However, the inquiries continued.

As we delved deeper into his affairs, the Panaji address given by Ingo to the RBI was found to be bogus. On inquiries with the RBI at Mumbai, it was found that by providing a fake address to obtain RBI's approval, Ingo had violated the Foreign Exchange Management Act (FEMA). Meanwhile, Ingo had approached the Goa High Court seeking relief as we had moved the local government for his deportation. Anticipating detention and deportation, he fled the country. We blacklisted him and got a lookout notice issued against him. If ever he tried to enter India, he would be arrested at the immigration checkpoint.

Ingo was never seen again in Goa. It is another matter that during my last visit to Goa I saw a flea market called 'Mickey's Night Bazar' in full swing, not very far from where Ingo had run his market!

* * *

In April 2006, the Indian cricket team was to play a one day international match against England at Fatorda Stadium near

Margao in Goa. Such events are commonplace in metropolitan cities, and police deployments are made for them as a matter of routine. Usually, the deployment pattern remains the same and is repeated. Goa was an exception to this. The last big event had taken place in 2001—five years earlier—when India had played Australia at the same venue. While the capacity of the stadium was 19,000, nearly 75,000 people had turned up to see the match, and they all had valid tickets. Apparently, the local organizers—the Goa Cricket Association—had printed that many tickets with total disregard for the stadium capacity or the repercussions of their actions. The inevitable followed with a stampede when the police had to use force to disperse the crowds desperate to enter the stadium. Somehow, the match was played, but the Goa Police, for no fault of theirs, came under heavy media onslaught. A commission of inquiry, chaired by Justice Pendse, a retired high court judge, was appointed. The Pendse Commission of Enquiry indicted the Goa Cricket Association for selling tickets far in excess of the capacity of the stadium.* The then president of the association and other office bearers were arrested for forgery and other charges.

I was naturally concerned and determined to prevent a repeat of the previous experience. To my horror, I learnt that the then president of the association was now the health minister of Goa and continued to head the cricket body. When we invited the office bearers of the association to discuss the proposed plans for the match with us, they were indifferent. When repeated requests fell on deaf ears, I decided

---

*   Pendse Commission of Enquiry

to report the matter to the Board of Control for Cricket in India (BCCI), the central body for cricket administration in India.

The match was still over six weeks away. I sent an email to the secretary of the BCCI explaining the situation. I reminded him of the earlier experience and requested that they direct the Goa Cricket Association to cooperate with us. The inquiry commission report indicting the office bearers was also attached to the email.

Within minutes of my sending the email, I received a phone call from the health minister's office. His secretary informed me that the minister wanted to see me immediately.

I realized in a flash that somehow the health minister had learnt of the email I had sent to the BCCI. He had found out that his mention in the email was not in complimentary terms. (I was to learn much later that the secretary of BCCI, on receiving the email, had promptly conveyed its contents to the board's president. Our health minister, in his capacity as the president of the Goa Cricket Association, was an ardent supporter of the president of BCCI and had voted for him in closely contested elections. The president, therefore, was beholden to the health minister and had considered it his duty to inform him about my email.)

By then I was wiser to the ways of the local politicos and told the minister's secretary that there was no way I would come to his office. I further added that I worked under the CM—who was also the home minister—and had nothing to do with the health minister.

As I had anticipated, within ten minutes or so, I received a call from the CM's office. Now the CM wanted to see me in his office. It was not difficult to understand that the health minister had complained about me.

As I drove to the CM's office, which was barely a five-minute drive away, I was determined to stand my ground and convey my point of view as aggressively as possible. If I went on the back foot I was sure to be clean bowled.

The office-cum-residence of the chief minister of Goa is located on Altinho Hill, arguably the best part of the capital city of Panjim. The neighbourhood, besides its good views over the city and the River Mandovi, is famous for the Bishop's Palace, an imposing structure built by the Portuguese. Right next to it stands a quaint old bungalow, which was the CM's camp office. The ground floor of the bungalow had offices for the CM's personal staff, while the first floor had his office chamber. Right across his office was a visitors' room, and in between was a narrow corridor. Both rooms had glass panels on their doors through which one could see what was going on inside.

As I stood in the corridor between the two rooms, I saw the CM in the visitors' room meeting a delegation of people. To my right, in CM's office, sat the scowling health minister, anger writ large on his face. I decided to walk into the CM's office, ready to take the bull by the horns. Even before I took my seat, the minister asked me brusquely, 'Did you take the government's permission before sending an email to an outside agency like the BCCI?'

I was quick to retort, 'I am the DGP of the state. When it comes to law and order here, I am free to do what I want. I don't need anyone's permission.'

My abrupt reply seemed to have the desired effect, and I could feel the minister squirm in his seat.

Meanwhile, the CM walked in. He seemed to be in a happy mood and inquired, 'I hope the matter has been resolved between you two?'

'Not in the least. The DGP is not relenting,' the minister lamented.

The CM, pointing to the minister and his aide, said almost pleadingly, 'DG sahib, he will do exactly as you want him to do. We all want a smooth conduct of the match. Please take him to your office. He will give you a written commitment to comply with all your terms and conditions. But please, withdraw the email you have sent to the BCCI. The minister's fair name is at stake.'

There was no need for me to press the point further. The minister and the secretary of the Goa Cricket Association accompanied me to my office. I spelt out the police's requirements and they were willing to meet all of them. They asked me to draw up a memorandum of understanding (MoU) between the Goa Police and the Goa Cricket Association, which I promptly did. They agreed to the printing of tickets—strictly as per the availability of seats in the stadium—under police supervision. Limited numbers of parking labels were to be issued depending on available parking space, and so on. Most importantly, the association was to cooperate with the police at every stage. The minister and his secretary signed the MOU without demur and I withdrew the email sent to the BCCI.

On 3 April 2006, as the match was in progress, I was happy to note that things had gone as per plan. Spectators had been seated without difficulty. Vehicles were parked in predesignated parking lots. No overcrowding or traffic bottlenecks were reported. Our arrangements had been successful.

Once things settled down, I decided to sit back and enjoy the game from one of the stands. To my pleasant surprise, the health minister came up to me and thanked me profusely for our well-planned deployment. Coming after the initial acrimony between us, his gesture was gratifying. We shook hands and hugged each other. This encounter with a Goa politico had come to a happy end. We met each other several times after, always warmly and cordially, until my tenure came to an abrupt end in October that year, with my transfer back to Delhi. I had spent all of eleven months in Goa, replete with skirmishes with local politicos—perhaps the reason behind my premature exit.

* * *

I am not sure if Goa is a microcosm of other Indian states where the police routinely work under the local political leadership. Maybe my experiences are nothing extraordinary, and my colleagues have faced even more harrowing situations at the hands of their political masters. But nonetheless, as these experiences sharply contrasted with my earlier experiences of dealing with politicians, I decided to pen them down for my readers. The next time you visit Goa, remember that behind the sylvan surroundings of the beach haven exists a seamy underbelly of unscrupulous elements in the garb of local netas, whom only true-life 'Singhams' and 'Simmbas' can keep in their place.

7

Moon-gazer

Moon-gazing is an esoteric pastime for a motley group of people ranging from celebrities to yogis. It is a part of Trataka, an ancient yogic technique that has been practised for thousands of years and is known to bring incredible benefits to those who practise it. It includes steady gazing at the moon that can apparently heal the eyes, clear the mind and even increase psychic abilities. Hollywood celebrities—Kate Hudson, for one—are known to have moon-gazing parties where invitees gaze at the moon for fifteen minutes and then meditate before their Rabelaisian pursuits commence.

I, too, by a quirk of fate, turned into a moon-gazer during the early years of my police career. Every evening as I returned home, I would look at the moon to see whether it was waxing or waning. Nights when the moon is down are called 'dark nights' in police parlance. It is on dark nights that criminals prefer to operate, as they are difficult to spot by police patrols. I would be anxious with the waning moon, apprehensive about the possible occurrence of a serious incident in my jurisdiction, as gangs belonging to an erstwhile criminal tribe were active in my district, whose depredations were the stuff of horror stories.

I was posted as deputy commissioner of police in south Delhi between 1989 and 1992. Midnight raids by gangs of criminals, who more or less had a common modus operandi, plagued my district. They would break into homes, bludgeon the residents to death in their sleep without any provocation and then ransack their homes, looking for jewellery, cash, wristwatches and other small items of value. If spotted and chased by the police, they would throw stones at them, sometimes severely injuring the officers, and then escape under the cover of darkness.

Usually sighted in their undergarments, they were commonly referred to as the 'kachchha-banyan' gang in police circles as well as in the media. Not much was known about their place of origin, their way of living and what made them habitual criminals and mindless killers. No database was available on them. Arrests, if any, were few and far between, with little effort to track their backward linkages.

The British, when they ruled our country, believed that certain communities in India were congenital criminals. Labelling them as criminal tribes, they enacted the Criminal Tribes Act in 1871, which, after several amendments, became the Criminal Tribes Act of 1911. Certain castes and communities branded as criminal tribes under the Act were subject to strict restrictions on their movements, required to report to the nearest police station on a weekly basis, and liable to search and arrest if found outside their prescribed area. On account of this 'branding' and stereotyping, the social ostracism, alienation and social exclusion of about thirteen million people belonging to 127 tribes followed.

When India became independent, this repugnant piece of colonial legislation, branding communities as habitual criminals and damning them forever, was repealed in 1949, and subsequently, criminal tribes were de-notified in 1952. This story is about a gang that belonged to one such erstwhile criminal tribe, whose members were identified, arrested and studied by us. By way of a disclaimer, it must be said that this story does not, in any way, suggest that people belonging to this de-notified tribe are habitual criminals or are not part of the mainstream social and national life. This account is only about those who, despite the passage of time and the government's efforts to wean them away from crime, were addicted to it, at least until their paths crossed ours.

* * *

On 12 May 1990, Mrs Veerawali, an eighty-five-year-old widow living alone, was found clubbed to death in her South Extension Part 1 residence, her valuables looted. This was in the jurisdiction of the district under my charge. I visited the crime scene and was appalled to see a poor old helpless lady bludgeoned brutally, her skull cracked open, blood and pieces of flesh splattered all over the walls, and her meagre belongings ransacked mercilessly. Having visited several crime scenes in my fourteen years of police service until then, I had fancied myself to be a tough cop who would not flinch when confronted with any crime scene. But I was not prepared for what was before me. Short of turning my eyes away and retching in front of my subordinate officers, I experienced every other revolting sensation during those moments. I recall steadying myself deliberately, lest I make a fool of myself before my juniors and the lady's relatives present at the spot.

During the preliminary investigation, what intrigued us was the probable motive to kill the old lady, who could easily have been overpowered and robbed. The main line of investigation, therefore, was based on the presumption that perhaps she recognized the intruders. This led to the theory that the motive to kill was possibly to grab her property, and the ransacking was done only to give the impression that this was a robbery. This line of investigation soon went cold when her immediate relatives, who could have staked their respective claims to her property, were found to be beyond reproach.

We had lifted fingerprints from the spot, but they did not give us any breakthrough either. They matched none in the Delhi Police database and we struggled with the investigation, probing misleading lines of inquiry. We were still in the thick of investigating Mrs Veerawali's murder when a similar incident occurred, not very far from her house, but in the jurisdiction of another police station of my district.

On 22 December the same year, as the day broke, I got a call from my district control room that a murder had taken place at R-12A, Hauz Khas. I rushed to the spot where the ACP, station house officer (SHO) and the local police station staff were already present. The scene of the crime was blood-curdling and horrific. Shraddha Khetrapal, a young and vivacious girl aged twenty-four, lay battered to death in her bed. The room had been ransacked and the poor girl's clothes and personal effects lay scattered all over the room. It was clear to us that this was a case of robbery with murder, much like the South Extension incident. Shraddha lived with her mother and brother in a spacious bungalow. Her room was on the ground floor, at the rear of the house, overlooking the kitchen garden. The premises had nothing to show for peripheral security and approaching the girl's room was easy. It was only a few steps from a public thoroughfare at the rear of the bungalow, across the tiny kitchen garden. All that was required to break into the room was to prise open the fragile latch on the inside of the bedroom door that opened into the garden.

Curiously, the victim's next of kin did not suspect robbery as the cause of her murder. They were quick to tell us that she had a paramour whom they didn't approve of, and it was he who must have killed her. But the crime scene investigation made it clear that the motive was robbery and robbery alone. Killing the poor girl was only incidental to facilitate the looting.

As we looked around the crime scene, I spotted a framed black-and-white photograph of the young victim smiling at us serenely, following us wherever we went. She was strikingly beautiful and looked full of life. The experience of rummaging through whatever was left of her belongings, while she had left this world forever, was rather unsettling and eerie.

We lifted fingerprints from the spot, which were sent to the bureau for identification. Lo and behold, some of them matched those retrieved from the Veerawali house. However, cross-checking with the Crime Record Office of Delhi Police revealed that the fingerprints did not match those of any known criminal on record. It was clear to me that a gang was active in my district and had already struck twice. That it would strike again, sooner rather than later, was almost a certainty. I was not prepared to see another such ghastly crime committed in my district and was determined to capture the culprits before they struck again. A sense of guilt had already begun to seep into me. Images of the battered heads of the old lady, and the pretty young girl who had yet to live her life, haunted me.

I addressed my officers and men in sampark sabhas (a term used in the Delhi Police to describe meetings between senior officers and their subordinates) repeatedly, exhorting them to take every possible measure to prevent the recurrence of such crimes. I held discussions with my officers, pored over maps of the district and its police stations, reviewed deployment and repositioned night pickets and patrols to block probable entry and exit points of the marauding gang in residential areas. Night watchmen and private guards of south Delhi colonies were included in the initiative and joint patrols started, particularly during dark nights. An awareness campaign in residential areas on dos and don'ts was begun. Care was taken not to create any panic. For four subsequent months, there was no repeat of the crimes. However, I must confess, I was cognizant of the vast spread of my jurisdiction, with its long borders with the Faridabad and Gurugram districts of Haryana, as also of the unlimited number of routes that the gangsters could take to access and exit the area. There was no way the district could be secured completely, regardless of the amount of manpower available. Fearing the

worst, particularly during dark nights, I was often gripped
by bouts of anxiety that kept me on my toes. I patrolled the
district, night after night, attempting to set an example for
my subordinates, who too spent sleepless nights.

Just when we thought we had made an impression on the
marauders and succeeded in keeping them at bay, they struck
again. On 18 April 1991, O.P. Mittal and his wife, both
over seventy, were found clubbed to death in their sleep on
the ground floor of their Panchsheel Park house. The crime
scene was as gory as the earlier ones left behind by the serial
killers. We didn't know where to look. By then the media had
begun to hound me, and justifiably so. Two senior citizens
had been murdered by a gang that had struck twice already,
and that too in a luxurious neighbourhood. Banner headlines
screamed across the front pages of newspapers the following
day, scoffing at us. Mercifully, we didn't have to contend
with TRP-hungry TV channels then, as the electronic media
was still in its infancy. Nonetheless, with the adverse reports
in the print media that followed these incidents, my bosses
had begun to show their displeasure with our inability to
prevent these heinous crimes. The psychological pressure was
mounting on me, and so was the sense of guilt and low self-
esteem.

Predictably, some of the prints picked up from the crime
scene matched those found in the earlier cases. Another glaring
similarity was that all three incidents had occurred during dark
nights. By now, I had seriously begun to follow the phases of
the moon. Come evening, I would compulsively look at the
sky to gauge the size and shine of the moon, whose waxing
and waning determined the quality of my sleep. During dark

nights I would invariably stay awake and organize 'general gasht' (patrolling by everyone) in the district, which meant that every last man in my district was out patrolling.

Then followed a hiatus of four months, again giving us the illusion that the worst was over. However, the gang was to strike again. On 11 August 1991, in the posh south Delhi residential colony of Saket, again under my jurisdiction, Major (Retired) Bakshi was found dead in a pool of blood with his head smashed. His house was ransacked and valuables looted. I was on serious notice now, but believe it or not, worse was yet to come.

* * *

Mausam Bhawan is the headquarters of the India Meteorological Department and is located on Lodhi Road in New Delhi. The road divides the south police district from the New Delhi district. The sprawling campus of Mausam Bhawan, however, was a part of the south police district and therefore under my charge. Though the building has an impressive facade, I never gave it more than a passing look while driving down Lodhi Road. That was soon to change, and change so much that even today, as I drive by, I cannot help but take a good look at it, a shiver making its way down my spine as I recall the gruesome crime committed in its precincts.

At the rear of the imposing building of Mausam Bhawan are located the residential quarters for its employees. On 28 January 1992, in one of these residential quarters, allotted to one Mr Saddy, the deadly gang struck again. Deepanshu

Saddy, a student aged eighteen, his sister Umang Saddy
and their mother Kamlesh Saddy were brutally attacked in
their sleep. While Deepanshu died on the spot, his mother
and sister were rushed to the hospital in critical condition.
Umang Saddy miraculously survived, but her mother
Kamlesh died of shock when she got the news of her son's
death.

Nothing could be more debilitating to the self-respect
and morale of a young police officer than visiting such crime
scenes. The sight of innocent people clubbed to death in their
sleep, their blood-soaked battered skulls, pieces of human
flesh and blood splattered all over, ransacked boxes and
cupboards, grieving and wailing next of kin, can make even
the most hard-boiled cop cringe. And the accusatory looks
from the family members of the victims and from members
of the public gathered at the spot can make you feel like the
culprit yourself. Every such case was a personal affront to me,
spurring my determination to solve these crimes and arrest
the perpetrators at the earliest.

Notably, soon after the Mausam Bhawan incident, a
member of the public spotted the criminals running away
and alerted a police patrol nearby. The police party chased
them and finding the policemen on their heels, the fleeing
criminals threw stones at them. Stones had also been found at
the scene of the crime at the Saddys' house. The use of stones
to keep policemen in hot pursuit at bay was going to become
the turning point in the war between the gang and the south
district police.

* * *

In the deep recesses of my memory lay the information that stones had been found tied to the waists of two criminals who were caught red-handed in 1989 in east Delhi's Preet Vihar area. I was then the DCP of the adjoining north-east district. It was quite often the case that criminals operating in one district operated in the neighbouring one as well. Regular sharing of information between the DCsP of the two districts was, therefore, a well-established practice. I was thus privy to the information that stones had been found on the person of the criminals involved in the Preet Vihar case. A number of heinous cases of armed burglary were worked out based on the disclosures made by the two arrested culprits. I also faintly remembered that, during their interrogation, they had disclosed that they were members of an erstwhile criminal tribe, about whom we had been taught in the National Police Academy.

The case file of the Preet Vihar crime was obtained from the east district and scrutinized. It came to light that the modus operandi in the said case was similar to that followed in the cases in our district, except for the killings. The criminals arrested in the Preet Vihar case belonged to Guna district of Madhya Pradesh.

In the absence of any other clue regarding the perpetrators of the serial killings in my district, I thought we had to approach the crimes differently from other cases of armed house robberies. These were criminals with completely archaic modus operandi who used stones and killed people in their sleep without any reason. Whenever sighted, as during the chase after the Mausam Bhawan incident and in the Preet Vihar case, they were found bare-bodied with only their undergarments or loincloths. Clues regarding them needed to be looked for, perhaps in their social customs and way of living. I felt their community had to be studied sociologically to get a breakthrough in investigations of crimes committed by them. The only place of their origin known to us was Guna in Madhya Pradesh, as per the case file of the Preet Vihar case.

I decided to send a young and resourceful officer to Guna, who would stay put there, make extensive inquiries with the help of the local police about the resident criminal gangs operating in Delhi and bring back as much information as possible on the de-notified tribe. I had to choose the officer carefully, and I made sure he was not serving in a police station. I was aware that officers serving in police stations would, on my orders, visit the place but would be in a hurry to get back to their regular jobs. I had to look for someone who had the necessary flair for fieldwork and the perseverance to look for that extra bit of information that would make the difference between failure and success.

A sub-inspector who had, until recently, been serving at the Pushp Vihar police post in my district was then in the reserve pool of officers in district police lines. I felt he would have the necessary desire to prove himself by completing the assignment given to him successfully. It was only a matter of time before the sub-inspector, Narender Chawla, proved that my choice was spot on.

* * *

Guna is one of the fifty-one districts of Madhya Pradesh. Its eponymous headquarters, located on the banks of the River

Parbati, is a small nondescript town, though on its outskirts are located an important industrial centre, a major fertilizer factory and a huge gas plant.

Maithali Sharan Gupt, a 1984 batch IPS officer, was the SP in the Guna district then. Before sending the sub-inspector to Guna I spoke to Gupt, informing him of the barbaric and macabre crimes being committed in my district and the suspected links with some of the criminals of his district. Even though I had never met him before (nor have I till date), when I requested him to help my officer in his field inquiries, he was extremely responsive. Aware that criminals from his district were operating in other parts of the country, the young SP ran his own chain of informers to keep tabs on them. He decided to depute the best from amongst these informers with my officer, the sub-inspector. Additionally, a crack detective of the district was also detailed with him to gather as much information as possible on local criminal gangs. The trio visited several villages that were known to have inhabitants with a criminal past, and my sub-inspector collected invaluable information on them. During his legwork, which took several weeks, he succeeded in creating a network of his own informers and studied the modus operandi of the criminals belonging to the erstwhile criminal tribe. He was, however, oblivious to the fact that he would soon do something small but so significant that it would prove to be the undoing of the gangsters.

Besides details on active criminals from Guna district who could be operating in Delhi, my sub-inspector brought back with him a sample of a 'daulatiya'—a multipurpose housebreaking-implement-cum-weapon-of-offence used by the criminals of the tribal community. 'Daulatiya', as the name suggests, means an implement that aids in earning 'daulat' (wealth). Made of wrought iron, it had a long handle with a sickle-shaped head and a short sharp tip on the top.

The daulatiya was shown to all officers and men of the south district in a specially convened meeting. Everyone was briefed that if the implement was found on any person or at the scene of a crime, a red flag should be raised immediately. Posters with images of the daulatiya were put up at all police stations and police posts as we geared up for the next cycle of dark nights.

On the night of 16–17 March 1992, a police party consisting of Constable Suresh Yadav (later promoted out of turn to the rank of head constable) and home guards Mohinder Singh and Vijay Kumar was patrolling the lanes and by-lanes of B block, Kalkaji, where thefts of car stereos were rampant. Constable Suresh Yadav kept an eye out for suspicious movements between the rows of cars parked in the dimly lit colony. He suddenly spotted four derelicts lurking among the cars. The constable alerted the two home guards and they tried to surround the suspects. The four miscreants, however, slipped away in different directions with one of them running towards the adjoining residential colony, Chittaranjan Park. The brave constable ran after him and saw him scale the 7-foot boundary wall of a bungalow and jump into its compound. The constable climbed on to the wall and probed the area along it with his lathi. He suddenly felt his long cane touch what felt like a human body. He signalled the home guards to enter the compound. Once face-to-face with the police team, the criminal whipped out a weapon and swung it at the policemen. The constable, an ex-wrestler, evaded the blow and succeeded in overpowering and disarming the criminal. To his horror, the policeman realized that the apprehended offender was carrying a daulatiya. A search of his person revealed stones tied around his waist. Constable Suresh Yadav immediately knew he had caught a prized suspect. He brought the culprit and his daulatiya to the Kalkaji police station with the help of the two home guards.

The significance of the arrest was not lost on anyone at the police station and the news was immediately disseminated to all concerned officers in the district. Arun Kampani, ACP of the subdivision, reached the police station and asked his best detectives to report to him post-haste. The interrogation of the arrested culprit was not an easy task. With great difficulty, he revealed his identity to the interrogators as Ramji Lal of village Naya Khera in the Jhansi district of Uttar Pradesh. He further disclosed the likely whereabouts of his companions who had escaped from the spot. ACP Kampani dispatched a police team promptly to nab the three culprits from Bata Chowk in Faridabad.

When the police team reached the likely hideout, they realized that the culprits had not yet arrived there. The cops lay in wait and after some time saw a few shadowy figures lurking in the vicinity. They were our quarries and were nabbed and brought to the police station in Kalkaji.

They turned out to be tough nuts to crack. Even to get them to tell us their correct names was a difficult task. It was thanks to the considerable skill used in the interrogation and our patience that they finally cracked. They finally owned up to being members of an erstwhile criminal tribe, having committed the murders of Mrs Veerawali, Shraddha Khetrapal, Mr and Mrs Mittal, Mrs Saddy and her son Deepanshu, Major Bakshi and a few other sensational murders from other districts as well. The gang leader of the arrested accused was Jodhan Singh aka Dadaniya of Babina in the Jhansi district of Uttar Pradesh. The stout, well-built gangster in his twenties was a monster. I still recall his interrogation in my presence after he had 'opened up'. While confessing to the killings in our cases, in a matter-of-fact and indifferent manner he said, '*Humney* Panchsheel Park *mein do insaan maare*, Hauz Khas *mein ek insaan*, Lodhi Road *par teen insaan*,' etc. (We killed two humans in Panchsheel Park, one in Hauz Khas and three on Lodhi Road.) For him, and perhaps his gang members, human beings belonged to a species different from theirs. They were remorseless and unrepentant about these killings. His able deputy was Anil Bharose, also from Babina, as was the third culprit Mohinder.

These disclosures made to the police led to the discovery of the stolen articles, and we were able to match the culprits' fingerprints with the prints picked up from the crime scenes in the above-mentioned cases. The accused told us the various places they had struck, which led to us solving all our sensational cases. Their interrogation and the follow-up fieldwork led to the creation of a huge volume of data on their modus operandi, their customs, habits, lifestyle and so on. Some of the details may be of interest to the readers.

The traditional occupation of these criminals was game hunting. This took them, in small wandering bands, to different parts of the country. At the relevant time, they were found in Andhra Pradesh, Maharashtra, Rajasthan and Madhya Pradesh. They operated around Jammu, Batala, Ludhiana, Delhi and Himachal Pradesh. They lived mostly in the vicinity of railway stations. They had very little by way of belongings and baggage. They were unkempt and dishevelled in appearance and roamed around barefoot. They believed that the goddess Devi had blessed them with immunity against insect or reptile bites. Their womenfolk and children usually stayed with them, aiding them in their crimes. Women wore long skirts with pockets and acted as couriers for the stolen property. The men masqueraded as balloon and plastic-flower sellers during the day and reconnoitred their area of operation carefully to select their targets.

Before setting out to commit a crime, a location where they could regroup was always decided upon so that in case they needed to disperse due to police intervention, they could reassemble at this spot. They committed crimes on dark nights after watching a late-night movie. Before setting out they removed their clothes, left them at the predetermined meeting point and then set out in their 'kachchha banyan' (undergarments). They usually applied oil on their bodies to make them slippery so that getting hold of them would be difficult. They tied stones to their waists, which could be used to attack police parties when chased. The leader of the gang usually carried a daulatiya.

The targeted dwelling was usually located next to a park or a deserted patch of land. Just before going for the kill, they would gather in the park or patch of land and wait until they felt the residents had fallen asleep. They would then break into the house stealthily. The daulatiya would be used to wrench out latches or iron bars installed in windows and doors. Small torches and drills were some of the other accessories that they would carry. Once inside the house they preferred to first kill the residents so that they could ransack the house unhindered. Killing the women of the house was not anathema to them as removing the ornaments from their bodies would be that much simpler. Sometimes, as in the Mausam Bhawan case, the stones tied to their waists were also used to attack and kill the sleeping residents.

Normally the criminals from this tribe looted cash and jewellery. If any one of them were caught red-handed, he would feign lunacy or drunkenness. If the charade was discovered and they were arrested, the police would find it hard to break them and get information out of them. The arrested criminal would never disclose his own name or that of his associates so as to allow his accomplices time to escape the local municipal limits.

The gangsters caught by us were all agile and fast runners. They would normally run away at superhuman speeds and were difficult to chase and catch. Use of coded calls to warn other gang members of danger was another feature of their modus operandi.

The arrest was a huge relief to us and to the public residing in south Delhi. The media was generous in its appreciation of our police work and we received favourable press. Some journalists wrote detailed accounts of our investigations and lauded the relentless efforts of the south district police. The officers of my team who had conducted the raids, arrests and searches, braving hostile and dangerous situations, were rewarded handsomely for their good work. These included sub-inspectors Avnish Dwivedi, Ishwar Singh, Suresh Kaushik and Narinder Chawla; and inspectors Raghubir Singh and Ajit Singh. ACP Arun Kampani supervised the operation commendably as I oversaw the investigations.

After nearly two years of facing media-bashing, untold stress and moon-gazing, we could now heave a sigh of relief and derive tremendous satisfaction from what we had achieved. In one go we had solved nine cases of housebreaking with murder and thirteen other cases from other parts of Delhi. Parties and social dos were organized within and outside the south district to felicitate us. We were over the moon, savouring the sweet taste of our success. Little did we know that our jubilation was to be short-lived.

On the conclusion of our investigation, during which we were able to recover substantial amounts of robbed goods and arrest other associates, the culprits were no longer needed by us for investigation and were therefore remanded to judicial custody by the court. They were, however, wanted by several other police teams, both in Delhi and outside. The first to get custody of the accused was the special staff of the neighbouring south-west district. Since their fingerprints had matched the chance prints picked up from the scene of an equally horrific crime committed on 18 November 1991, wherein retired Major General O.P. Kalhan and his son Surender Kalhan were murdered in their sleep in Delhi Cantonment, the accused were interrogated by the police of the south-west district, and as further investigation was still under way, they were lodged in the lock-up of the police station in R.K. Puram.

On the night of 20–21 April 1992, only a month after their arrests, the phone in my bedroom rang in the dead of night. It was ACP Kampani. The news he relayed to me jolted me out of my bed and shocked me out of my wits. Jodhan Singh alias Dadaniya and Anil Bharose—the two kingpins of the gang—had escaped from the lock-up of the R.K. Puram police station. Kampani reported that they had used the lid of the cistern in their cell to make a hole in the poorly constructed wall of the lock-up and escape. The police guard posted outside was oblivious to what was going on inside the cell and realized what had happened a bit too late.

I sat on my bed, staring at the phone in disbelief and sincerely hoping it was all a rude joke or a horrific nightmare. Despair and impotent rage overtook me as the telephone kept shrieking incessantly. I could see the triumphant face of Jodhan Singh having the last laugh.

How could anyone have allowed this to happen? Why did the south-west district not have adequate security around the lock-up? Why had Singh and Bharose been held like ordinary criminals and how could anyone be so careless? The questions that crossed and agitated my mind were many. But there were no answers to them.

Naturally, front-page stories with mocking photographs of the gaping hole in the lock-up of the R.K. Puram police station appeared in the newspapers the following day. It was an embarrassing moment for the Delhi Police. Facing the next of kin of those who had been butchered by Singh et al. was very difficult. The two desperados had proved that they were veritable Houdinis, difficult to keep in captivity for long.

I immediately dispatched police teams to Babina in Uttar Pradesh and Guna in Madhya Pradesh to check if the fugitives had gone there. But our searches and raids were all to no avail. The hunt for Singh and Bharose began all over again.

It was clear to me that pertinent information, if any, would come from Guna and Guna alone. I had kept in touch with Maithali Sharan Gupt, the SP of Guna, who alerted his informers of the escape and the urgency of arresting Singh and Bharose. The SI was once again dispatched to Guna to make inquiries in the villages inhabited by the gang members and alert his own informers. We waited with bated breath for any information about their whereabouts.

* * *

Having completed three full years in the south district I had moved to the Crime Branch of Delhi Police in the first week of August 1992. Meanwhile, the case connected with the escape of the two gangsters from the R.K. Puram police station had been transferred to the Crime Branch. In my new assignment as DCP of the Crime Branch it was my responsibility to take the case to its logical conclusion by tracing the gangsters who had escaped from police custody.

Luckily, maintaining contact with the SP of Guna paid off. Within a month of the 'great escape' of the serial killers, informers of the Guna Police spotted Singh and Bharose near Chak Murania village in Guna district. They had taken refuge in the jungles on the outskirts of the village and were being provided succour by their associates Tataria and

Babla, who lived in the village. The Guna Police planned to raid their hideout, but the felons got wind of the impending raid and ran away. However, their associates Tataria and Babla were arrested. Sometime later, another informer spotted Jodham Singh, alias Dadaniya, in Varanasi and tipped off the Guna Police. A joint police party comprising policemen from the Guna and Varanasi police forces arrested Jodhan Singh near the Adampur police station in Varanasi. When the SP of Guna informed me of Singh's arrest, I was over the moon and greatly relieved. SI Ishwar Singh, who, like me, had moved to the Crime Branch from the south district, was deputed to take custody of Jodhan Singh from the Varanasi Police and bring him to Delhi. The Crime Branch party arrived in Delhi with the rearrested gangster on 25 August 1992.

Jodhan's rearrest made headlines in Delhi newspapers. The local media, which had sensationalized the escape, was impressed by our efforts, made in tandem with the Guna and Varanasi police, to trace the escapee. Interrogating Jodhan gave us vital clues on the likely whereabouts of his associate Bharose. Soon, in a joint raid conducted by the Crime Branch and the south district police, Bharose was also apprehended from the jurisdiction of Bari Bareilly in the Raisen district of Madhya Pradesh, thereby restoring the lost prestige of the Delhi Police.

Jodhan Singh and his gang were tried and convicted in the cases against them. Investigations had revealed that hundreds of their clansmen were operating all over the country, though not all of them were as senselessly violent as the gang headed by Singh.

This was a unique investigation as studying the customs, modus operandi, history and social mores of the tribe to which this group of criminals belonged led to the breakthrough in the heinous cases. It is not often that such an approach is adopted to solve a crime.

Our study showed that this tribe of traditional hunters was at some stage used by Chhatrapati Shivaji as guerrillas to harass the Mughal armies. The Maratha chief utilized their intimate knowledge of the topography of the Deccan Plateau and their hunting skills to his advantage. It appears that once the wars between the Marathas and the Mughals slowly abated, the tribesmen were left to fend for themselves. But the instinct to kill, which they had acquired while fighting the Mughals, continued to haunt them and was possibly what led them to commit such crimes.

When British rule ended in 1947, the Government of India, in an effort to integrate the tribe into mainstream society, allotted twenty-five bighas of land to each family. However, by then, they had taken to crime habitually— mainly burglaries and robberies. They gave away the land allotted to them on 'batai' (share-cropping) basis to traditional farmers.

'That the criminal belonging to this community is addicted to crime is undeniable—he does not labour, he cannot and would not stop, his hands are as soft as any clerk's and prove he does no manual labour in the fields which he sometimes might profess to do,' observed a British police officer who had dealt with these criminals.

Some of the gang members have amassed considerable wealth from crime and have acquired huge landholdings as

large as 250 bighas, with tube wells and tractors. Despite
their prosperity, they travel to far-off places, to commit
crimes. They stay on railway station platforms, footpaths
or parks in squalid conditions. However, when they return
home, they wear good clothes and ornaments, watch films
and consume meat and alcohol regularly.

The villages inhabited by these gangs are laid out in a
manner that makes it difficult for the police to raid them.
Usually, houses are built at an elevation, surrounded by
jungles, canals, rivers or rocky outcrops. While doing research
in the Guna district, SI Narinder Chawla discovered that an
observation post ('machaan') is a common feature of these
villages. Members of the tribe take turns as watchmen, whose
job it is to alert the villagers if they notice a police party
approaching the village. The village has a well-established
contingency plan. The inhabitants dig ditches around the
village, which work as a moat. If a large police party is seen
approaching the village, water from the tube wells is released
into these ditches, thereby cutting the village off from the
approach road. The womenfolk intercept the policemen at a
safe distance from the village and engage them in animated
conversation, allowing the criminals enough time to swim
across the moat and disappear into the jungles. If the
police party is small, the villagers do not hesitate to attack
it. Members of this criminal community, after committing
heinous offences, rush to their deras (temporary camps)
where they quickly weigh the stolen jewellery and count the
cash. The women then conceal the booty in their long skirts
and return to the village. Out of the booty, the lion's share

(25 per cent) is taken by the gang leader and the remaining is divided amongst every member of the gang, including the leader, equally. Thus the leader gets an equal share over and above his 25 per cent. They also have regular receivers of jewellery to whom the booty is sold.

I collated the findings of our study into two monographs that were in great demand then, not only within the Delhi Police but also by the law enforcement agencies of neighbouring states that also regularly suffered from the crimes committed by the marauders.

Sustained preventive efforts made by the Delhi Police and the forces of the bordering states had the desired result, and gradually, crimes committed by these gangs abated.

More importantly, no incident in which sleeping inmates were killed and their houses robbed recurred in the capital of India. Thus came to an end the depredations unleashed by Jodhan Singh and his gang in Delhi. Our painstaking efforts had borne the desired results, much to our satisfaction and to the maintenance of peace in the area. My moon-gazing gradually came to an end.

With the steady passage of time, residents of Delhi have all but forgotten—and naturally so—about the serial killings coupled with robberies that once plagued the city. Given the public's short memory, millions of Delhi's citizens born in the 1990s and thereafter in the new millennium may not have even heard of the marauding gangs who killed people in their sleep before ransacking their homes.

Today, we, the citizens of Delhi, sleep soundly, hardly aware of the dangers that lurked during dark nights in the early 1990s. Don't we owe a tiny bit of gratitude to those officers and men of the Delhi Police who tracked down and arrested these dangerous criminals from far and wide and booked them nice and proper, thereby terminating their depredations?

8

Night of Shame

It was 10.20 p.m. on 16 December 2012. The incessant traffic on National Highway 8 between Delhi and its satellite city, Gurugram, refused to abate even though it was well past peak hours. Wave after wave of speeding vehicles sped on the highway like swelling waters gushing in a river in spate. A light smog hung in the air, occluding light from the already dim street lights from reaching the road, making the atmosphere seem dark, eerie and sinister. The biting cold of Delhi winter was yet to set in, but for two youngsters—one male and one female—who had been lying by the roadside without a stitch of clothing on them for almost forty minutes, it was chilling to the marrow.

Raj Kumar and his partner Surender Singh, of EGIS Infra Management India Ltd, a firm charged with the maintenance of the national highway, drove slowly in their jeep in the left lane of the highway from Gurugram to Delhi. They were looking for stretches in disrepair that might need the attention of their superiors. As they crossed the U-turn under the Mahipalpur flyover, they heard cries of '*bachao, bachao*' (help, help) from the left flank of the road. They were startled to see a young man and a young woman sitting naked, covered in blood, shivering and writhing in pain. They immediately stopped and called Rampal Singh in their company's control room, informed him of what they had seen and requested him to call the police.

Rampal Singh lost no time in calling the Delhi Police control room (PCR) on the emergency telephone number, 100, which dispatched the nearest PCR van, Zulu 54, to the spot. With its shrieking siren and flashing emergency lights, the emergency response team reached the spot in no time. As Head Constable Ram Chander and his staff approached the site, they saw a motley crowd of bystanders surrounding the naked young couple on the ground, with no one making any attempt to help. The youngsters were bleeding profusely and were visibly in pain. The police team dispersed the crowd, brought a bottle of water and two bed sheets from a nearby hotel for the couple, and quickly covered them to save them from the cold and the voyeuristic gaze of the onlookers.

The police team rushed the severely injured couple to Safdarjung Hospital, which was about 10 kilometres away. En route, the injured, despite being in a state of shock, narrated snatches of their nightmarish ordeal to Ram Chander, a summary of which he passed on to the central PCR.

On arrival at the hospital, the male victim, by then identified as Awindra Pandey (aged twenty-eight), was admitted to the casualty section of the hospital. The female victim, Nirbhaya (a name given to protect the identity of the girl and universally accepted) (aged twenty-three), was taken to the gynaecology department as her private parts were bleeding profusely.

The PCR had by then informed DCP Chhaya Sharma of the incident. Realizing the gravity of the situation, she rushed to the hospital. Dr Sachin Bajaj, who was treating Awindra, had already heard from his patient the details of the ordeal the victims had been through. In brief they were as follows:

Awindra, an engineer, and his girlfriend Nirbhaya, a physiotherapy intern, had gone to the Select City Walk mall in Saket in south Delhi to watch the movie *Life of Pi*. After the show they exited the mall at around 8.30 p.m. Unable to get an autorickshaw to Dwarka, where they lived, they took one to the Munirka bus stand from where they hoped to get a bus that would take them to their destination.

On reaching the Munirka bus stop, they waited for their bus—number 764—to arrive. After a while, they saw a white bus with yellow and green stripes on its sides approach them and stop right where they stood. It was a private chartered bus—generally not authorized to ply on commercial routes—from which a young boy was calling out for passengers going to Dwarka and Palam Mod. Awindra and Nirbhaya, unsure of when the regular bus would come and anxious to reach their homes before it got too late, decided to board the private bus. Little did they know they had boarded a bus to hell.

As they took their seats they saw three unkempt youngsters sitting in the driver's cabin with the driver, while two others sat right behind in the front row of passenger seats—one on the left and the other on the right end. There were no other passengers in the bus. Instinctively, the young couple felt that something was not quite right.

One of the two seated in the front passenger seats walked towards Awindra, ostensibly to collect the bus fare. They paid twenty rupees between them. It dawned on them that the bus had not waited for any other passenger to board and had left with only the two of them, soon after they had got in. Strangely, the bus had curtains that were all drawn to ensure that nothing outside was visible to them. The door they had come in through had been locked from the inside after they had boarded. The eerie atmosphere soon became outright scary when the lights of the bus were switched off. The two youngsters knew they were in trouble.

As the bus drove towards Dwarka and reached the flyover leading to the airport, the three boys emerged from the driver's cabin. They began to abuse Awindra, asking him where he was taking the girl so late in the night. On being told by Awindra that it was none of their business, one of them punched him in the face. Nirbhaya and Awindra retaliated to the verbal and physical abuse hurled at them. In the commotion that ensued, they heard one of the goons call out the names Vinay and Pawan, commanding them to bring out iron rods. Soon Awindra was hit on the head and legs with iron rods and he fell to the floor of the bus. As blows rained on him, his mobile phone, his wallet containing a thousand rupees, his wristwatch, credit cards and the clothes he was wearing, including his shoes, were all taken away.

Nirbhaya shouted for help and tried calling the police on her mobile. The hooligans pounced on her like a pack of hungry wolves, but she fought them with all her might. She was pushed to the rear end of the bus and then pinned down on a passenger seat meant for three, where all six men took turns to rape her. As punishment for her fierce resistance, she was hurt grievously with iron rods in ways so gory and sordid that I will refrain from describing them to my readers. She too was robbed of her belongings and was stripped naked. Having satiated themselves, the men decided to get rid of the injured couple, and if possible, kill them. Awindra heard one of the assailants say that the couple was not to be left alive.

They first attempted to throw them out through the rear door of the bus, but it refused to open. A naked Nirbhaya was then dragged by her hair to the front door and thrown out along with her companion, who was also without a shred of clothing on him. The bus tried to reverse and crush them to death but somehow the two managed to roll away and escape. The spot where they were found was roughly opposite Hotel Delhi 37, one of the many small motels and boarding houses along the service road heading towards Gurugram. What stands between the hotel and the spot is the Mahipalpur flyover with its various arms.

*　*　*

I was then posted as the commissioner of police, Delhi, and was barely six months into my assignment after thirty-six years in the police force. This was going to be my last assignment before I retired. I certainly wished to sign off after a successful stint. Little did I know that the most testing time of my career was to come within six months of my taking over as the chief of Delhi Police.

The news reached the control room at my residence in real time. The wireless operator on duty that night woke me up. The information given to me then was sketchy, and since DCP Chhaya was at the scene, I felt reassured and tried to go back to sleep. However, I was restless for the rest of the night, checking on developments in the case every now and then.

At the hospital, DCP Chhaya heard the shocking details of the case from Awindra, particularly about the way Nirbhaya had been assaulted and the kind of injuries inflicted on her. She met Nirbhaya in the ICU and saw her pitiable condition. She was appalled and traumatized as never before in her career. The DCP found it difficult to come to terms with the extent to which Nirbhaya had been violated and brutalized by those depraved men.

No matter how much we in the police are trained and exposed to ghastly crimes, mutilated bodies and the brutish side of mankind, there are some moments in our careers when human weakness gets the better of us. It is to DCP Chhaya's credit that she pulled herself together, collected her wits and continued with the job at hand.

Based on the details given by Awindra about the bus in which the horrific crime had been committed, DCP Chhaya sent out a wireless message through the central PCR for all PCR vans and police patrols to look for a white bus with green and yellow stripes on it. Border check posts were alerted to intercept white buses matching the description.

She then went to the Vasant Vihar police station with Awindra, and based on his statement, registered a case of rape, abduction, armed robbery with attempt to murder and entrusted the investigation to SI Pratibha Sharma.

The DCP realized that this was, in Delhi Police jargon, a 'very bad case', and she had to take swift action. In the absence of any worthwhile clues, she knew that if the case was to be cracked, locating the bus was critical. All that was known from Awindra's account, besides its colour and the stripes painted on its sides, was that it had a separate driver's cabin, red seat covers and yellow curtains, and that the hubcap of the front left wheel was missing.

She summoned the ten best inspectors of the south district to the Vasant Vihar police station with their respective teams. Inspector Rajender Singh of the Special Staff—an experienced and versatile officer—was the star investigator amongst them. DCP Chhaya allocated specific jobs to each inspector and made the police station her mission control room. None of them went home for five days and nights, not until the last accused had been arrested.

One team left for the Delhi Transport Department to get details of all white buses registered with them. Transport department officials were woken up and pulled out of the comfort of their beds. By about 5 a.m., the police had the details of 320 white buses. The team began to look for these buses and their owners that were based in Delhi, as well as for other white buses at the bus terminals in neighbouring states.

Another team led by SI Pratibha Sharma, the investigating officer on the case, completed formalities at the hospital and visited the spot where the two youngsters had been found. She collected samples of bloodstained grass and leaves from nearby bushes, dirt soaked with blood and so on and sealed them securely.

Inspector Rajender Singh and two other teams scoured the CCTV footage from all hotels and guest houses on the national highway opposite the crime scene. Interestingly, the police teams noticed a white bus with 'Yadav' painted on its side in the CCTV footage of Hotel Delhi Airport. The bus was seen coming from Delhi, seemingly heading for Gurugram, but within nineteen minutes, at 9.53 p.m., it reappeared on the screen, heading again in the same direction. The obvious conclusion was that it had taken a U-turn from under the flyover located close by, proceeded towards Delhi instead of going towards Gurugram, and had again turned around to drive towards Gurugram.

The CCTV footage of the white bus was shown to Awindra, who confirmed that it indeed looked like the bus he had boarded. He looked intently at the front left wheel, and sure enough, it did not have a hubcap. The search for the white bus had now zeroed in on those that had Yadav written on their side.

By then several transporters and bus owners with white buses had been questioned. With the additional information that they now had to look for a white bus with Yadav written on its side, the police search became more focused. The teams began to question the transporters if they knew anyone who owned buses with Yadav written on their vehicles. During these inquiries the name of one Dinesh Yadav of Noida, a city in Uttar Pradesh, came up. He owned a fleet of buses, most of which had his surname written on them. When questioned, Dinesh confirmed that he did indeed own a bus that had red seat covers, yellow curtains and Yadav written on its side. The bus, as disclosed by him, was on charter with Birla Niketan School in Saket. He further disclosed that the driver was named Ram Singh and lived in one of the shanties of Guru Ravi Das Camp, a slum abutting Sector 3 of R.K. Puram in south Delhi. The driver usually parked the bus in the vicinity of his abode.

By then it was 11 a.m. on 17 December, the day following the crime. A police team rushed to Guru Ravi Das Camp and saw the bus parked there. On inquiries, two local residents, namely Brijesh Gupta and Jiwat Shah, came forward to testify that they had seen two men cleaning the inside of the bus late at night. They had also seen the men burning clothes. On inquiring where the bus's driver resided, the jhuggi was found and Ram Singh (aged thirty) was nabbed, despite his best efforts to escape. He took the police team to the bus, which was inspected in the presence of witnesses. It had been washed from the inside and every effort made to obliterate all traces of evidence. A forensic team was called, which recovered two bloodstained iron rods, a debit card in the name of Asha Devi (Nirbhaya's mother), traces of blood, hair and spit from inside the bus. A T-shirt and a pair of bloodstained brown slippers were also seized. Ram Singh further led the investigating officer to the spot where he had tried to burn the clothes of the victims. SI Pratibha Sharma collected the ashes and pieces of unburnt cloth from the spot. On closer inspection, a UNIX mobile phone and an MTNL SIM card were also found and seized. After the forensic examination and the seizing of articles with evidentiary value, the bus was moved to Thyagaraj Sports Complex for safe custody, away from the glare of the public and the media.

Despite the seizure of the bus and other pieces of incriminating evidence, Ram Singh, when brought to the police station, denied his involvement in the crime. He first refused to participate in the test identification parade

before Awindra. He tried to pass on the blame to his brother
Mukesh, who, he said, had taken the bus the previous evening
without his permission. On being asked about Mukesh's
whereabouts, Ram Singh said he had run away to their village
in Rajasthan. But, we had a piece of evidence of Ram Singh's
involvement that he could not rebut. His mobile phone data
showed that he was in Hauz Khas at 9.16 p.m. for thirteen
seconds, then at Vasant Gaon at 10.04 p.m. for fifty-one
seconds and again at the same location at 10.06 p.m. for
twenty-five seconds. These were spots on the route taken
by the bus, as per the investigation made thus far. When
confronted with this evidence, he admitted to having driven
the bus but maintained he was not a party to what may have
happened at the rear of the bus.

DCP Chhaya ordered his medical examination. Bruises
were found on his body and blood on his clothes. A cast of
his teeth was taken and his jaw photographed. The bite marks
found on the body of the female victim were to be matched
with the cast of his teeth and the bloodstains on his clothes
were to be DNA fingerprinted with the blood of the victims.

It was only at 4 p.m. on 17 December—the day after
the crime—that Ram Singh (aged thirty-four) accepted his
involvement and gave a graphic account of the sequence
of events. The details given by him matched Awindra's
statement. He was placed under arrest, and I received
information of the breakthrough from Vivek Gogia who was
the joint commissioner of police, Southern Range. In fact,
I still remember exactly where I was when I received the
message. I was on C Hexagon near India Gate, on my way to
the Ministry of Home Affairs (MHA) in North Block.

On the evening of 17 December I received a call from Sonia Singh of NDTV, who asked me rather curtly, 'Mr Kumar, don't you think you should resign from the post of commissioner of police in view of the horrific incident of gang rape?'

Until then I had been monitoring the developments in the case calmly, pleased with the recovery of the bus, the arrest of the first accused and the unravelling of the mystery behind the crime. Sonia Singh's brusque question jolted me. I wondered why a senior journalist, who was usually quite affable and personable, and was from a respected channel, would ask for my resignation. We had always shared a cordial relationship, and she was the first media person to interview me after I had taken over as commissioner of police. Indeed, a horrific crime had taken place, and I, as police chief, was as upset as, if not more than, anyone else. My officers and men were working overtime to resolve the case. We had already made a significant breakthrough during our overnight investigation and had arrested an important accused. No police failure on any count was evident. On the contrary, the response of the PCR, the pace and methodology with which the bus had been traced and the first accused arrested by the south district police were developments that everyone should be pleased with, I thought to myself. But the focus seemed to be on why the crime took place at all.

A reasonable answer to this question could be that the safety of women in Delhi has always been a sore point with the citizens of the national capital, and understandably so. The common perception is that women are not safe in public spaces in Delhi. A girl walking along a road or in a marketplace is often the victim of men staring at her lecherously, making suggestive comments and catcalls, and on some occasions, even physical outrage of her modesty. In public transport, groping hands or deliberate body contact is not infrequent. To add to all this, shocking incidents of rape and murder are reported from time to time. But the rape and assault of Nirbhaya was a case apart in terms of its sheer brutality.

* * *

Ram Singh's interrogation revealed the involvement of his brother Mukesh (aged twenty-six), his neighbours Pawan (aged nineteen) and Vinay (aged twenty), his bus cleaner Akshay Kumar Singh (aged twenty-eight), and lastly, a youngster he knew as Raju (name changed as he is a juvenile in conflict with the law). Raju, according to Singh, was gifted in hailing passengers in a unique manner and was popular in the bus transport community of the trans-Yamuna area or east Delhi.

On the evening of 17 December—the day Ram Singh was arrested—SI Arvind Kumar of the Special Task Force of the south district left with a police team of six for Karoli in Rajasthan, 300 kilometres away from Delhi. His mission was to nab Mukesh, Ram Singh's younger brother. The police team drove all night and reached Karoli in the wee hours of the following day. The policemen from Delhi reported to the Karoli police station the following morning (propriety demands that a police team from outstation inform the local police of their arrival and the purpose of their visit to the local jurisdiction). SI Arvind requested the local police for additional forces. He was told that he would have to wait until at least 10 a.m. for local police help. The police team was pressed for time and was in no mood to wait. SI Arvind, as the team leader, lodged an entry in the police station daily diary noting his arrival and left for Mukesh's village, which was 40 kilometres away.

The village was 2 kilometres away from the nearest road, and the approach to it was not motorable. The police party had to cover the distance on foot. The hut in which Ram Singh and Mukesh's parents lived was not in the main village but in the middle of an agricultural field, a little distance away. What stood between the police team and the hut was a river with neither a bridge across it nor any ferry service. The police team realized that they would have to swim across it. One member of the team, a consummate swimmer, was sent in advance to check how deep the river was. Luckily, it was crossable, but there was one difficulty—the AK rifles and pistols the policemen were carrying would have to be protected from being submerged in water. Undeterred, the policemen stepped into the icy waters of the river with their weapons raised above their heads. A few of them were not tall enough to keep their heads above water and had to walk on their toes.

As they approached the hut, dawn was breaking. Fortunately, no movement was seen outside the hut. The residents seemed to be asleep inside. The team encircled the hut and raided it. Mukesh, who had been hiding out with his parents, was caught unawares. The police team, with Mukesh in custody, had to cross the river again and hurry to their vehicles. Luckily, since Mukesh's hut was at some distance from the main village, the other villagers did not learn of the arrest. The police party, without wasting any time, drove back to Delhi.

By the morning of 18 December, news of the unfortunate incident had reached the media and quite expectedly, spread like wildfire. Crowds began to collect at the Vasant Vihar police station, comprising mostly members of the media, representatives of non-governmental organizations (NGOs), students of Jawaharlal Nehru University and some local people. They raised slogans against the police and prevented policemen from entering and leaving the station. However, the police team continued to interrogate Ram Singh even as the slogan shouting outside became deafening. DCP Chhaya had to come out to brief the media gathered outside and share some details of the investigation done thus far to assuage the rising tempers.

Much before SI Arvind reached Delhi with Mukesh on the afternoon of 18 December, Ram Singh had begun to sing like a canary. He disclosed that in the early evening of 16 December (a Sunday) Pawan Kumar, a fruit vendor, Vinay, a gym instructor, Mukesh, Ram Singh's younger brother, Akshay Kumar Singh, a cleaner on Ram Singh's bus, and Raju, a juvenile, met in his jhuggi and had a small 'party'. They decided to set out together in Ram Singh's bus to have some 'fun'. They first lured Ram Adhar (aged thirty-five), a carpenter, to board the bus and robbed him of Rs 1500 along with his other belongings and dumped him near IIT Gate. They then drove towards Munirka from where they picked up the hapless couple.

Ram Singh then pointed out Pawan's hutment in Guru Ravi Das Camp from where he was picked up at 1.15 p.m.

on 18 December. Vinay was arrested from outside his gym, again in Ram's neighbourhood, at 6 p.m. the same day. The data from both Pawan's and Vinay's phones corroborated their presence along the route that the bus had taken. We had four of the six accused in our custody. It was time for us to let the world know of the breakthrough in the case and of the arrests we had made.

A press conference was called at police headquarters on the evening of 18 December. The anti-police stance of the media was palpable when I addressed the press to inform everyone how deftly the case had been worked out, that four accused had been arrested, and that the remaining two were likely to be arrested soon. However, my statement didn't cut any ice with anyone present. On the contrary, the body language of the press reporters, with whom I had always had cordial relations, had suddenly changed. It was a foreboding of things to come.

With my coming to the forefront by addressing the media, the focus of the public shifted from the Vasant Vihar police station to the police headquarters. Quite a few from amongst the crowds, on learning of the four arrests, were of the view that it was now time to show solidarity with the rape victim and pray for her rather than protest. They gathered at India Gate with lit candles and placards against rape, demanding safety for women. As it always happens in such situations, riding on popular sentiment, political groups were getting involved and the crowds continued to swell. A certain party, harried by charges of large-scale corruption, thought it was the right time to divert public attention and began to participate in the protests. Lumpen elements, as is their wont, joined the otherwise peaceful crowds, making them belligerent and offensive.

In a way it was good for our investigation that the police station in Vasant Vihar was no longer under siege and the police team there could now move about easily. But officers working at the police headquarters, particularly I myself, found it difficult to reach and leave our offices. We often had to play cat and mouse with the by then not-so-decent press persons to evade them.

Sharing information about our successes in the investigation and the four arrests failed to make any impression on the crowds that continued to swell outside the headquarters. India Gate was another venue where largely young people began to gather in large numbers to demonstrate peacefully.

At around this time, a senior politician's son demanded my resignation on TV. This was quickly followed by his parent's demand for the same. When the protestors heard of these demands, they quite naturally took the cue and joined the chorus. Very soon, it became a campaign not so much against the Delhi Police but against me. Both in print and electronic media, the speculation centred on my ouster. On one occasion, when asked why I refused to hand in my resignation papers, I replied, 'I am not a quitter. Indeed a most ghastly crime has been committed under my charge. My job is to ensure that all culprits are arrested and brought to trial. As long as the government has faith in me, I will continue pursuing the case and not turn my back.'

The following day, a leading newspaper carried the banner headline that I had refused to quit, implying that the most logical thing for me to do in the situation was to leave, or for the government to sack me. And here I was, with no business to continue as commissioner of police, refusing to budge from my seat. My mobile phone was inundated with messages—both text and WhatsApp—asking me in vulgar and nasty language to quit. My family members, particularly my daughters, were threatened with dire consequences, including rape. The poor girls, realizing that they should not add to my woes, kept this information to themselves and shared it with me only after the storm had blown over.

Nobody was prepared to come out on any platform and defend us; there was no one to say that it was no fault of ours and that we had done well to crack the case so quickly. Neither any political leader in the government nor any senior bureaucrat in the home ministry was willing to tell the public that the police had responded to the situation professionally. On the contrary, it was a free-for-all. A retired senior colleague of mine, whom I respected very much, wrote a centre-spread article titled 'Sack Him' in a renowned newspaper. Though he has since passed away, I have kept the press clipping with me until date, as a reminder of those trying days.

On the evening of 18 December, the chief minister of Delhi convened a meeting of the heads of various non-governmental organizations working for women's security and welfare. Women activists, including a few eminent lady advocates, were invited to the meeting and so was I. I took Dharmendra Kumar, my special commissioner of police (law and order) along. The meeting, we soon realized, had been convened to allow the invitees to vent their grievances and criticisms on how the Delhi Police had failed to protect the women of Delhi. It appeared to be a competition in who could punch the police harder. Both Dharmendra and I felt as if we stood before a firing squad with endless ammunition. I kept my cool up to a point, but when the proceedings became a bit too much, I reciprocated in equal measure, following which there was a relative amount of order. The meeting had clearly been held more to run us down than serve any constructive purpose.

Later that same evening, I was summoned by the Union home minister to his residence. He asked me, 'Why is your CM staunchly against you? Today she came to see me with a large delegation of her MLAs to demand your ouster.'

I had no answer for this as I thought that she and I had shared a good relationship all along.

I left the minister's office and during my drive home, I called the CM. Her private secretary, A.K. Tripathi, answered and put the CM on the line.

Respectfully, I asked her, 'Madam, what is it that you hold against me? I invited you to my daughters' weddings and you most graciously attended both. We as a family have called on you and you were so nice to us. You too have been to our house for get-togethers. Suddenly, what has happened that you want me out?'

'You have taken action against only constables and head constables and none against senior officers,' she mumbled.

'Who told you that I have taken action against lower subordinates? No such thing has happened. Why should I take any penal action against anyone? Because they have solved the case, because they arrested the accused? If I had touched any one of my people, who would work on the case?' I retorted.

There was some more mumbling at the other end and she hung up. Till date, the reason why she turned against me is a mystery.

The lieutenant governor of Delhi, Tejendra Khanna, was on vacation, visiting his brothers in the US. When he heard the news of the rape he decided to cut short his sojourn and returned to Delhi on the night of 18 December. The following morning, despite his long journey and jet lag, he reviewed the situation with us at Raj Niwas and called for a press conference. He highlighted the good work done by the police in the case thus far and assured everyone that the remaining accused would be arrested shortly. But the reporters would have none of it. They wanted to know when the commissioner of police would be sacked. The lieutenant governor told them that there was no reason for the government to remove me. He generously pointed out that the person whose blood they were baying for had distinguished himself throughout his career with his good work, and the question of sacking him did not arise. I was present during the press conference and was overwhelmed when he told the press reporters, almost chidingly, 'Do any of you know that on account of his excellent work during the Commonwealth Games, he was invited by the UK government to assist them in organizing security for London Olympics?' Pin-drop silence followed the lieutenant governor's reprimand. I was touched by what my immediate superior had to say about me.

I would soon realize that various forces were at work behind the scenes. First and foremost was the long-standing demand of the Delhi government to bring the police under its control. Even though Delhi was given statehood in 1991, some important departments such as the police and the Delhi Development Authority (DDA), which deals with land, are under the lieutenant governor. This duality has always been a bone of contention between the Delhi government and the Central government represented by the lieutenant governor, who is appointed by the Government of India.

Clearly, the forces seeking control over the police were in overdrive to capitalize on this incident and get the police under their charge. Ironically, at the time of this unfortunate incident, the state government and the Central government had the same ruling party. The demand for full statehood continues till date, as does the conflict of interest between the state government and the lieutenant governor. The December rape case became a useful handle to malign the prevailing system wherein the Delhi Police are under the lieutenant governor.

Another unseen force at work was a personal enemy of mine—a powerful bureaucrat of the Central government, someone I had booked for corruption while I served in the CBI. He had been under suspension ever since my team had arrested him in 1999. He had done his best to block my appointment as the commissioner of police. Luckily, he had not succeeded in his designs. This horrific case gave him the opportunity he had been waiting for.

Several pseudonymous complaints, ostensibly made by former civil servants and an eminent advocate, addressed to the president of India, with copies marked to all and sundry, started making the rounds. They all had one demand: sack the commissioner of police. When the addresses of the complainants were verified they were found to be in existence, but nobody by the senders' names lived there. These complaints were similar to the ones circulated when I was being considered as a prospective candidate for the post of commissioner of police and earlier, for empanelment for the post of director of the CBI. The suspended bureaucrat had succeeded in prejudicing the then chief vigilance commissioner, who was the chairman of the selection committee to shortlist candidates for the post of director of the CBI. As was conveyed to me later by more than one member of the committee, the chief vigilance commissioner had prevailed on the committee that my inclusion would lead to a public uproar!

That is the power of false propaganda and false complaints in government, or for that matter in public life. All you need is a committed and vengeful detractor with a word processor. If he has a couple of celebrity accusers to support him, as my sworn enemy had in an ageing advocate and a prominent politician, then you've had it. They can make the most preposterous and frivolous complaints against you, but before consigning these petitions to the dustbin, the system demands they go through 'due process'. These complaints will invariably end up on your desk and you will spend your lifetime responding to them and pleading your innocence. You are always on the back foot defending yourself and it is up to your seniors to accept your explanations or reject them. The irony is, even if your defence is accepted, the onslaught of these complaints leaves an impression in the back of your superiors' minds that there must be something wrong with you. At every stage of your career—be it promotions, foreign trips, grant of awards, empanelment, etc.—these complaints return to haunt you. You pay a heavy price for discharging your duty by taking legal action against powerful people.

The unscrupulous bureaucrat lodged bogus complaints against me in every conceivable forum—the prime minister's office, the MHA, the Central Vigilance Commission (CVC), the Delhi government, the office of the lieutenant governor et al. I have lost track of how many hours I spent responding to them.

Coming back to the case, it was brought to my notice that the suspended bureaucrat had used some of his ill-gotten wealth to bankroll the outrage directed at me—both in the higher echelons of the media and in political circles. He joined hands with the political forces inimical to the Delhi Police and financed the protests to a large extent. I cannot fully substantiate my allegation for my readers, but an insider privy to this conspiracy shared its details with me shortly before I retired. He rang me up, identified himself as a lawyer and insisted I meet him. During the meeting he confessed that he, with a few others, had been behind every complaint filed against me, at the behest of the dishonest bureaucrat. Of late, he had fallen out with the bureaucrat as the latter had played dirty with him. He wanted to let me know that a lot of money had changed hands between the dishonest public servant and the local political leadership of the day with my ouster being the ultimate goal.

(As we go to print, the bureaucrat has been compulsorily retired by the Government of India. Charges of corruption and extortion against him are some of the reasons cited by the government for this drastic measure. This restores my faith in karma and divine retribution.)

* * *

Around this time, a nascent political party with its roots in Delhi had lost steam and was gasping for breath after its supreme leader, who had mass appeal, decided to call it quits. The December rape case provided the dying party with yet another opportunity to take to the streets to revive and reassert its existence. Its party workers constituted a major portion of the crowds demonstrating against the government of the day and demanding my ouster.

While the protests and demonstrations raged in the city, the media, particularly the electronic media, was full of anti-police rhetoric. I felt it was important for me to take the brunt of the attacks myself and insulate my team working on the case. I had many an unpleasant encounter with star TV anchors, but the good thing was that their misplaced aggression ended at my doorstep. The team working on the case could focus on the investigation without having to deal with the media.

* * *

From the accused Ram Singh the role of Akshay Kumar Singh aka Thakur had come to light. Akshay worked with Ram Singh as a cleaner of the bus. Ram Singh knew the mobile number Akshay called to speak to his family back home. He shared the number with the police; it was registered with a service provider

in Aurangabad, Bihar. A team under Inspector Rituraj was
dispatched by air to Patna on 18 December. The inspector
contacted Pradeep Kumar Shrivastava, inspector general of
police, Special Branch, Bihar, who was a distant relative of his.
Inspector Rituraj shared details of the case and requested the
local police's cooperation in arresting Akshay from his village.
Instructions were immediately passed on to Aurangabad's SP
and filtered down the official hierarchy, all the way to the last
rung. Inspector Rituraj hired a Scorpio SUV and drove from
Patna to Aurangabad with his team. They reached late on the
night of 18 December and camped out in a motel.

On 19 December, the Delhi Police team established
contact with the staff of the police station in Tandwa, in
whose jurisdiction Akshay's village was located. The area
was affected by left-wing extremism and the police station
in Tandwa had been attacked four times by Naxalites in the
recent past. The station was therefore heavily fortified, with
personnel from the Bihar Military Police deployed on its
rooftop, armed with light machine guns. SI Ajay Kumar, the
young officer in charge, against official instructions not to
venture out after sunset, came forward on his own to join the
Delhi Police team. They planned to recce Akshay's village
stealthily so as not to alarm its residents.

Local inquiries revealed that Akshay was not in the
village. He had most likely gone to visit his in-laws, who also
lived in a Naxalite-affected area. Inspector Rituraj's team,
on the advice of SI Ajay Kumar, decided to lie in wait. The
inspector did well to keep the chowkidars of the village—the
eyes and ears of the local police—in the loop. He promised
them a handsome reward if they helped him nab Akshay.

On 21 December, Akshay was spotted by a chowkidar getting off from a train at Tandwa railway station and then walking towards his village. The chowkidar lost no time in informing Inspector Rituraj, who rushed with his team and arrested Akshay. The news of Akshay's arrest was conveyed to us before noon on 21 December.

Inspector Rituraj needed to obtain a transit remand from the local court in order to take Akshay to Delhi. Whenever the police make an arrest in an area outside their own jurisdiction, the law requires the arrested person to be produced before the local court of law and a transit remand to be obtained. The arrested person can then be lawfully produced before the court concerned. Inspector Rituraj contacted the district magistrate (DM) of Aurangabad to request his help in obtaining the transit remand at the earliest. The DM informed him that the district judge was attending a party at his residence and that the inspector should come there. Inspector Rituraj reached the DM's residence and was introduced to the district judge, who took him to his residence, summoned his staff, dictated the order and issued a transit remand. By then it was 9 p.m., but the Delhi Police team decided to leave at the earliest for the nearest airport, which was in Varanasi.

There was a dense fog that night, which afforded poor visibility. Against the advice of the SP, Aurangabad, not to drive in such dense fog, Inspector Rituraj left for Varanasi with the accused and his team. On the request of the inspector, the SP provided a police escort to accompany the Delhi Police team to the Bihar–UP border. The visibility on the road was barely seven to eight feet. The driver stuck to the centre of the road to keep track of where they were going and inched towards Varanasi—176 kilometres away—undeterred.

The police party along with Akshay reached their destination in the early hours of 22 December and took the first flight to Delhi at 9.15 a.m. They reached Delhi airport at noon, and from there Akshay was taken directly to the court and his police custody remand taken.

We now had the fifth accused in our custody. The Union home secretary, R.K. Singh, was pleased with the progress in the investigation and decided to call a press conference in the Ministry of Home Affairs.

The media continued to be hostile. The fact that the Union home secretary was addressing the press conference and speaking well of the Delhi Police was unacceptable to them. At the end of the conference, I heard snide comments from the press reporters. Their ire was also directed at the Union home secretary, who had spoken well of the police, and they alluded sarcastically to the fact that since both he and I were from the same state, the home secretary was taking a soft stance towards the police. Not a single reporter was ready to acknowledge the good work done by the police or the weight of my heavy stare.

Raju—the juvenile in conflict with the law—was the only accused left to be arrested. He was the one who had hailed Nirbhaya and Awindra at the Munirka bus stand to board the bus.

Ram Singh had disclosed that Raju had stayed with him on the night of 15 December—the day prior to the crime. The two knew each other as they had worked together two years earlier in the trans-Yamuna area.

The police did not know Raju's real name, his cellphone number or his address. None of the other accused knew anything about him.

In the absence of any specific clues, the police went to the trans-Yamuna area, which has a population of 50 lakh in a 50 square kilometre area. It was much like looking for the proverbial needle in a haystack. Police teams fanned out in the area and started asking for a boy named Raju at various bus depots located in east Delhi. Stray bits of information about him came from some quarters alluding to his rapid changes in occupation. He may have been a ragpicker, then a fruit seller and then moved on to bus-cleaning jobs. No one had any specific information on him. The persons who claimed that they had met Raju were requested to be part of the search teams to identify the boy. The search for Raju continued for three days and nights.

Finally, a local resident, who had joined the police search for Raju, spotted a youngster who he thought was Raju in a bus plying between the Anand Vihar bus terminal and Noida. The search then zeroed in on buses plying that route.

On the morning of 21 December, the spotter identified Raju on a bus returning to Anand Vihar from Noida. As soon as this information was relayed to the police, a team rushed to the Anand Vihar bus station and nabbed the juvenile. With Raju's arrest, all accused involved in the dastardly crime were in our custody.

However, the demonstrations at India Gate and Raisina Hill refused to abate. The composition of the crowd was amorphous and diverse with no one leader who could be approached by the government to initiate a dialogue. Nor was any political leader of standing prepared to come forward and address the protestors on behalf of the government. It was a stalemate between the police and the protestors, who wanted to make Vijay Chowk a Tiananmen Square of sorts.

On the afternoon of 22 December, the cabinet secretary of the Government of India, Ajit Seth, convened an emergency meeting attended by Pulok Chatterjee, the principal secretary to the prime minister, and senior representatives of the Intelligence Bureau (IB) and MHA. I was also present along with Dharmendra Kumar, my special commissioner of police (law and order). As the meeting was in progress, news of protestors at Raisina Hill turning violent reached us. Even though all the six accused had been arrested, the wrath of the demonstrators was difficult to assuage.

During the meeting, everyone wondered what the protestors were looking for after the arrest of all accused. While various opposition parties and lumpen elements wished to keep the embers burning, there wasn't anything left to be done by the government. I took the liberty of telling those present that crowd psychology usually expects victory for itself in some form or the other, some takeaway to show that their protests were not in vain. It was my assessment, based on the feedback from my officers dealing with the protestors on a day-to-day basis, that they expected the government to strengthen the laws dealing with crimes against women. Secondly, they wished to know if there had been any failings on the part of the police, and if so, those responsible should be punished. I proposed that judicial committees should be appointed to go into both these aspects. I was aware that by offering to undergo a judicial inquiry, I was sticking out both my own neck and those of my boys.

Pulok Chatterjee remarked, 'The prime minister would not be willing to accept the proposal. He believes that the police have done their job well and having any inquiry against them is out of the question.'

Cabinet Secretary Seth said that since the proposal had come from the police chief himself, Chatterjee might consider speaking to the prime minister again.

Within a couple of hours, news reached me that the prime minister had acquiesced in our request, and soon orders were issued appointing a judicial committee, headed by Chief Justice (Retired) J.S. Verma, to study the existing laws dealing with crimes against women and to propose amendments, if any. Justice (Retired) Usha Mehra was to head another committee to conduct a judicial inquiry to determine if there had been any lapse on the part of the police or any other government agency in preventing the crime and responding to it.

Contrary to our expectations, even after the government's announcement regarding the appointment of the two committees, the protesters refused to relent. India Gate and Raj Path continued to be under siege by the protestors. The Russian president Vladimir Putin was scheduled to visit Hyderabad House—only 75 metres away from India Gate— for a state banquet the following day, a fact everyone in the home and external affairs ministries was jittery about.

By the late afternoon of 23 December, the crowd at India Gate turned violent. Stones were hurled at the police and police barricades broken. The unruly elements, who had by then hijacked the protests, uprooted barricades being installed for the Republic Day Parade, which was to take place a month later, and made a bonfire of the wooden poles. They began to use the iron pipes of the barricades to attack policemen. They overturned an official car of Doordarshan—the government TV channel—and set it on fire. The police used hundreds of tear gas shells and fired water cannons repeatedly, but the crowds stood their ground. With the impending visit of the Russian president at the back of my mind, I was getting impatient. Given the law and order situation in the vicinity of the venue, there was no way the official function could have been held there. I knew something had to be done sooner rather than later to disperse the crowd and bring some semblance of order at India Gate.

Both Dharmendra and I were in the C4i (command, control, communications, computers and intelligence) centre of our PCR monitoring the proceedings, which were being streamed live by our own CCTV vans stationed at India Gate. Acts of arson and attacks on policemen were being flashed repeatedly on the screens. I told Dharmendra it was time to disperse the unlawful assembly.

'If the officers at the spot are hesitant to do so, let both of us go to India Gate and do it,' I shouted.

Dharmendra pacified me. He said, 'Sir, we will get it done from here itself.'

Orders were given rather harshly to Taj Hassan, the joint commissioner heading the police deployed at the spot, to disperse the mob post-haste, and if necessary, use force.

The police resorted to lathi charge and the crowd dispersed in less than an hour after severe clashes with law enforcement. In this operation, many demonstrators and policemen were injured. Head Constable Subhash Tomar of east Delhi, deployed at India Gate, was beaten up mercilessly and died subsequently at Lady Hardinge Medical College Hospital.

Regrettably, the media showed no remorse or sympathy for the late head constable or his bereaved family. They tried to pass it off as a death caused on account of the head constable's poor cardiac condition and not the injuries he had sustained at the protestors' hands. Neither the media nor the citizens of Delhi were willing to show any sympathy, leave alone respect for a policeman who had died in the line of duty. For most of us, and particularly me, it was a painful and shattering experience.

The only silver lining was that, besides the government benefits to the family of the slain head constable, in a fine gesture, the iconic and legendary film star Amitabh Bachchan sent a handsome amount of money by cheque, with a letter of condolence to the bereaved family. While no citizen from the city of Delhi, some of whom have vulgar amounts of wealth, came forward to help the late head constable's kin, at least a celebrity of the stature of Bachchan, living over a thousand miles away, deemed it his duty to recognize the policeman's martyrdom and chip in to help his family. I was touched by his gesture and sent him an emotional thank-you letter on behalf of the Delhi Police.

* * *

Post the clean-up operation at India Gate, the next big task was to ensure that the protestors did not occupy it again. To seal the many approach roads to the monument on a round-the-clock basis was a humongous task. The government was unable to provide additional force, and consequently, we had to make do with our own resources. We had to virtually close down our police stations and draw out every single man for deployment. Policemen set up barricades on all approach roads to the central vista to prevent demonstrators from reaching it. The credit for this unprecedented mobilization and deployment goes to Dharmendra Kumar.

I would often meet my men braving the cold in the dead of the night, share a cup of tea with them and try to raise their morale. It is to their credit that after 23 December, crowds were not allowed to gather anywhere near India Gate.

* * *

In the interim, Nirbhaya's condition continued to deteriorate. It was decided at the highest level in the government to shift her to Singapore for better medical care. On 27 December she was flown in an air ambulance to Singapore and admitted to Mount Elizabeth Hospital. Despite everyone's best efforts and her brave battle for life, Nirbhaya breathed her last on 29 December. An autopsy was performed by a coroner's court in Singapore. Her mortal remains were brought back to Delhi and cremated by her parents at Dwarka under heavy police cover. Needless to say, from the moment the body arrived to the time it was cremated, the atmosphere in the city was tense and we were all on tenterhooks. Numerous police officers at different levels put their best foot forward to ensure that everything was peaceful.

The next big challenge was to file a charge sheet for the case at the earliest. The longer the case was pending investigation with the police, the longer wild speculations and rumour-mongering would carry on. However, preparing a charge sheet was not easy. Evidence related to the case was scattered in files and in the case diaries of several investigating officers. Similarly, scientific evidence in the form of forensic, medical and technical data collected during the investigation had yet to be collated. All the data had to be pieced together carefully and marshalled to establish a direct and unbreakable link between the crime and the criminals. Vivek Gogia, the joint commissioner of police, Southern Range, informed me of his intention to get this work done and prepare the charge sheet within ten days. I was happy to learn that my team could achieve this difficult target in such a short while. Vivek and DCP Chhaya, ably assisted by Pramod Kushwaha, inspectors Rajender Singh, Atul Kumar, Anil Kumar and several others including the investigating officer Pratibha, did an excellent job of preparing the charge sheet and filing it in court within ten days of the last arrest.

We engaged Dayan Krishnan, a noted senior advocate of the Supreme Court, as our chief prosecutor. I had known him since my CBI days and didn't need to look any further. A low-profile lawyer with tremendous legal acumen and unimpeachable integrity, we couldn't have found anyone better. For Dayan Krishnan, it was not just another case, but a mission he was setting out on. Not many people are aware that the distinguished lawyer took the case pro bono and did not charge the government any money. Rajeev Mohan— another veteran public prosecutor—assisted Dayan ably.

The legal team vetted the charge sheet, and I asked to review it before it was filed in court. It is a matter of considerable professional contentment for me that I not only contributed to the presentation of the evidence in the case, but also pointed out some major lacunae that, if not made good at that stage, could have created serious issues during trial.

Finally, the charge sheet of the case was filed on 3 January 2013. After the completion of mandatory legal requirements, the trial commenced on 5 February the same year and was held on a day-to-day basis. A special team, headed by Inspector Rajender Singh, was deputed exclusively to assist the prosecutors. A total of eighty-five prosecution witnesses and seventeen defence witnesses were examined. The doctors in Singapore who had treated Nirbhaya and the coroner who had conducted the post-mortem were examined and cross-examined in the court through videoconference, perhaps the first time in our legal history that such a thing was done.

* * *

When I look back on the high points of those trying times, the fieldwork done by the detectives of the south district during the nights of 16 and 17 December 2012 to identify and locate the bus using CCTV footage of hotels in Mahipalpur stands out as a remarkable piece of police work. I shudder to think of the consequences if the initial breakthrough had not been made so quickly. Following the initial breakthrough and the arrest of Ram Singh, Pawan and Vinay, the three field operations conducted to arrest the remaining accused, namely, Mukesh, Akshay and Raju by 21 December were outstanding. Looking for Raju with no knowledge of his real name, address, physical appearance, the details of his employer or even his religion was an exquisite piece of fieldwork done by the police team headed by SI Arvind Kumar.

Use of criminal forensics and technical data were other high points in the out-of-the-ordinary investigation conducted in the case. Careful collection of evidence from the spot where the male and female victims were found, from the interior of the bus and elsewhere, and the use of DNA matching of blood, hair, saliva, etc.; the matching of bite marks on Nirbhaya's body with the dental casts of Ram Singh and Akshay; the use of cellular data to establish that the accused and the victims were together in the bus on the route it took; the CCTV footage from Select City mall to show that the couple had seen a movie there and had left by 8.30 p.m. on 16 December; the CCTV footage from Hotel Delhi Airport to prove that the bus had passed it twice within a span of nineteen minutes; the dying declarations of Nirbhaya; the testimony of the eyewitness and the medico-legal experts, all made it a watertight case. Pleas taken by the accused in their defence were countered with irrefutable physical and scientific evidence at every stage.

The trial concluded on 9 September 2013 holding the accused guilty of, amongst other things, rape, armed dacoity and murder. They were all sentenced to death, except for the juvenile who was sent to a reformatory for three years. The verdict was, subsequently, upheld by the Delhi High Court on 13 March 2014 and the Supreme Court of India on 5 May 2017.

On 10 March 2013, Ram Singh, the prime accused, committed suicide in Tihar Jail. Until then, he was an undertrial and had been held in judicial custody. The remaining four, namely, Pawan, Vinay, Akshay and Mukesh, await hanging.

A closer look at the social background of the rapists is revealing. They all come from more or less the same kind of social milieu. They are all migrants from the Indian countryside to the city; unskilled or at best semi-skilled; poorly educated or not educated at all; in search of employment; living on the brink of survival by doing petty jobs that give them just about enough to put some food on their tables, and ironically, money to recharge their mobile phones; they are all unmarried or separated from their families and therefore sex-starved. This class of deprived men live in cities, dazzled by the wealth they see around them—sleek cars, shiny malls, palatial homes, super de luxe hotels and, most appealing to them, young girls smartly turned out. This is not only true of the capital city but of every metropolitan city in India. At some level, we have to recognize this reality of the stark juxtaposition of the two classes and the dangers that inevitably emerge from it. Police forces in such cities, contrary to public expectation, find it difficult to be omnipresent at all times to prevent sexual crimes by such brutes.

In this case, the victim's father was also a migrant from a remote village in Uttar Pradesh, who moved to the city in the early 1980s in search of employment. He took up sundry jobs until he was engaged as a loader at the Delhi international airport. He married soon after and the couple had three children—Nirbhaya, the eldest, followed by two sons. Nirbhaya performed well academically and aspired to be a neurosurgeon. However, she settled for a more affordable four-year course in physiotherapy in Dehradun. Her father had to sell his land in the village and liquidate all his savings to raise the Rs 40,000 required to secure her admission in the physiotherapy institute. She graduated with flying colours and was awaiting placement when the tragedy struck. Nirbhaya represents an aspirational India that wishes to make a mark by dint of hard work, education and acquiring skills. She will be remembered not only as the victim of a horrific crime but also as an aspirational Indian woman, whose life was cut short by ruthless criminals.

* * *

Some incidents and cases are watershed moments in the history of not only a police force, but also the city where they occur and possibly even the country. The anti-Sikh riots in Delhi, the terror attack on the Parliament House and the 26/11 terrorist strikes in Mumbai are such cases. The Nirbhaya case, as the brutal Munirka bus rape case is commonly referred to, was another such tipping point. It galvanized public opinion on the issue of crimes against women and the laws to deal with them not only in India, but worldwide. We in India did well to rise to the occasion and amend our laws drastically by introducing the Criminal Law (Amendment) Act, 2013, amending the Indian Penal Code, Evidence Act and Code of Criminal Procedure with respect to sexual offences. For the first time, offences such as sexual harassment, voyeurism, acid attacks and stalking were expressly recognized and criminalized.

Following these developments, there is empirical data to show that more women are coming forward to report sexual offences committed against them. The most welcome change is that women in India are finding their voice following the Nirbhaya case. They talk about their daily travails in dealing with men, both in public and private spaces, and come forward to report crimes. A cynical view persists in some quarters, though, that nothing has changed after the bus rape case of 2012.

The Nirbhaya case led to an outcry that changed our laws and made them stronger with respect to crimes against women. The focus of the public wrath was the criminal justice system, and particularly the police. Pitched battles were fought between the protestors and the police in which several on both sides were injured and one policeman even lost his life.

In over 96 per cent of rape cases and crimes against women the perpetrators are known to the victims.* Most crimes of this nature are committed within the four walls of homes or offices, by close relatives, colleagues and friends. Should we not pause and ponder if blaming the government or the police for these crimes is the most sensible thing to do? Doesn't the cure for this malaise lie elsewhere? Will endless police-bashing help the situation in any meaningful way?

Undoubtedly, those were trying times for the Delhi Police in general and for me in particular. But this cannot possibly be compared to the trauma and tragedy that the

---

* National Crime Records Bureau 2016, data table 3, A.4, p. 147.

victim and her family suffered. The public outcry was natural, but regrettably, the situation got politicized and lumpenized, as such cases always do. As far as the police response was concerned, at the end of it all, we emerged stronger and wiser. This case was yet another befitting example of how the Delhi Police can stand up to challenges competently and promptly.

At a personal level, I feel privileged to have been at the helm of affairs in the Delhi Police and to have led my force during such adverse circumstances. That I succeeded in keeping the investigation team insulated from the wrath of the media by taking the brunt of the attack myself—running the risk of being made a scapegoat and being thrown out in disgrace at any moment—was a matter of great professional and personal gratification. The exemplary manner in which officers measured up to the challenges of this case, on both the investigation and law and order fronts, was equally heartening. Filing of the charge sheet in 10 days of the incident, the piecing together and marshaling of physical and scientific evidence, effective prosecution in the courts of law and getting the accused convicted were extraordinary achievements by the force. They did so in the face of two judicial inquiries, hostile public opinion, bad press and several PILs filed in superior courts. They went about performing their work with equanimity and courage that kept my head held high and proud.

Finally, it must be acknowledged that the Government of India and the lieutenant governor were steadfast in their support of the police. They stood by us like a rock, and this prevented our morale from waning. The then Congress president and the prime minister met groups of protestors at their residences, even after midnight, to pacify them. Such

support from a government in power for its police, in the face
of adverse media and public sentiment, is commendable and
exemplary.

At the end of it all, this story is first a tribute to brave
Nirbhaya, whose promising life was cut short in a barbaric
manner. We do not know to what extent we have succeeded
in getting her justice. Perhaps history will give the final verdict
in this matter several decades down the line.

Equally, this story is a salutation to Head Constable
Subhash Tomar, who lost his life in the line of duty at the
hands of unruly elements at India Gate on the evening of
23 December 2012. Last but not the least, no amount of
words can ever express my appreciation and gratitude for the
officers of the Delhi Police, who stood by me in those trying
times and delivered what was expected of them brilliantly.

As I now reflect on the case and the testing aftermath I
faced, I am reminded of the words of the American author
and publisher Orison Swett Marden.

The *Success* magazine founder Marden said: 'Success is
not measured by what you accomplish, but by the opposition
you have encountered, and the courage with which you have
maintained the struggle against overwhelming odds.'

Indeed, his words have held true for me throughout my
policing career, as they did in this case.

9

Sovereignty under Siege

The day fedayeen militants from Pakistan attacked India's Parliament House, I was in my office at the CBI headquarters in New Delhi. Television crews covering the Parliament beat captured parts of the attack—the most daring yet in Indian history—live. Little had the broadcasters reckoned that instead of interviewing political personalities that morning they would have to report on a 9/11-type attack, which had incidentally taken place only three months before in New York. Many of the cameramen themselves were scurrying for cover as gunshots rang in the air and bullets burst out of automatic weapons from all directions, killing several policemen, a lady police constable, two Watch and Ward staffers and a gardener. The fedayeen militants were dangerously brainwashed members of the same freelance jihadi groups that were looking for an opportunity to strike at important symbols of governance and finance all over the world, united in their heavily misplaced belief that high-profile killings were the only way to find a permanent solution to their never-ending grievances. Alas, they are yet to realize that terror never wins. The footprints of these diabolical men, seized with a burning desire to blow themselves up and exchange their lives for those of hundreds and thousands of innocents, can now be traced to all major terror attacks across the world including, as I write, in Sri Lanka. New Delhi on 13 December 2001 was no exception.

Delhi's winter may not have turned bitterly cold yet, but the nip and bite in the air was quite sharp. However, the wintry air had little to do with the chills that ran up and down my spine as I stared, shell-shocked, at the news channels, the gesture resonant of my actions after 9/11, when I had watched the aerial attack on New York's twin towers unfold live. Never in my worst nightmares had I thought that the Indian Parliament would one day be attacked, and that too by armed men in battle fatigues from another country.

Had it not been for the presence of mind and rapid action of some valiant policemen and parliament staffers, many of India's celebrated political leaders may not have escaped from harm's way. One of the fedayeen militants, who was blown to smithereens, was only yards away from entering the main hallway of the Parliament. Had he succeeded in getting in, anything could have happened, for, like the others, he was armed with the deadliest and latest automatic weapons and had enough ammunition to engage our security personnel for hours.

The incident gained international attention in a matter of minutes, thanks to the presence of foreign media channels in Delhi. Weeks later, India primed itself for war against

Pakistan, whose territory had been used to train and launch the terrorists.

Before proceeding further, a word or two must be said about the beautiful and structurally perfect architecture and layout of the Parliament House (Sansad Bhawan), located in the heart of New Delhi. This will help the readers gain a better understanding of the crime.

Designed between 1912 and 1913 by the architects Sir Edwin Lutyens and Sir Herbert Baker, its circular shape was possibly inspired by the Ashoka Chakra. It is 171 metres in diameter and colonnaded with 144 columns. The Duke of Connaught laid its foundation stone in 1921 and Lord Irwin inaugurated the building in 1927. The imposing building is surrounded by large gardens with fountains and a sandstone wall along its perimeter. The total area of the parliament estate is 6 acres (approximately 2.5 hectares).

In its central edifice are twelve gates with porches that serve as entry points to the building. Gate number one is the main entry point for MPs, their support staff and visitors. The gates are numbered anticlockwise. As one enters the parliament precincts from the Sansad Marg (Parliament Street) side—the direction the terrorists came from—gate number one falls on one's right. If one proceeds further around the central edifice, the next two gates are twelve and eleven. It was gate eleven where the action started on that fateful December morning.

Three agencies, namely, the Delhi Police, the CRPF (Central Reserve Police Force) and the Watch and Ward staff look after the security of the Parliament House. The outer cordon is the responsibility of the CRPF, the inner cordon of the Delhi Police and the isolation cordon (inside the building) of the Watch and Ward staff.

* * *

It was a pleasant morning in Delhi on 13 December 2001. The winter sun was out but shone feebly. For most citizens of the city and their elected representatives it seemed like the perfect winter morning. Given an option, they would have preferred to sit out on the lush green lawns of any one of the city's splendorous gardens, munching peanuts or reading a newspaper and soaking in the sun. But the languorous mood was soon to change.

Both the Rajya Sabha and the Lok Sabha had adjourned at 11 a.m., though many parliamentarians and a few ministers, including the home minister, were still inside the Parliament House. Forty minutes later, five heavily armed terrorists in a white Ambassador—most official cars then were of the same make and colour—displaying stickers of the home ministry and Lok Sabha on its windscreen, entered the Parliament House complex through one of the iron gates opening on to Sansad Marg to the north. The security staff deployed at the entry point was either lax or was taken in by the stickers that were displayed and failed to intercept the vehicle. Truth be told, nobody had anticipated such an attack, and therefore the premises lacked security overlays (such as bollards, boom barriers, etc.) and the security deployment that exists today, after the incident. 'It is easy to be wise after the event,' said Arthur Conan Doyle. Today, the Parliament House is a veritable fortress, but alas, it was not so that December morning.

The terrorists, once inside the complex, drove undetected and unhindered along the circular edifice of the building, in a clockwise direction, at breakneck speed, until they ran into a dead end created by nearly 2.5-metre-high wall. The wall stood about 20 metres ahead of gate eleven, the entry point to the parliament precincts meant exclusively for the vice president (VP) of India, who is the ex-officio chairman of the Rajya Sabha. The VP's car was parked in the porch, and his security detail and driver were waiting for him to come out. Finding themselves in a cul-de-sac—something they had not anticipated—the terrorists had to bring their car to a screeching halt.

The terrorists, who presumably must have received exhaustive briefings about the layout of the Parliament House from their handlers, did not seem to be aware of the wall. The terrorist driving the car tried to reverse out of the dead end and in his nervous haste hit the front right side of the VP's car. The VP's chauffeur, Shekhar, who was standing close by, shouted at the driver and with SI Shyam Singh, Assistant Sub-inspector (ASI) Jeet Ram and ASI Nanak Chand of the VP's security detail, almost simultaneously and instinctively, rushed to the offending vehicle. It was then that the five occupants of the car emerged from its four doors and opened fire. ASI Nanak Chand was hit and died on the spot, while ASI Jeet Ram was severely injured. Dressed in battle fatigues, the assailants looked like army commandos—well built, carrying AKs, backpacks slung over their shoulders, and ready to do or die.

Curiously, until then, no one had really noticed anything odd about them or their rash driving within the parliament estate precincts. As the terrorists emerged from the car, brandishing their weapons and firing indiscriminately, it dawned on the security men that a terror attack was under way. The first thing that the Watch and Ward staff did was to shut all entrances into the building. Quickly, personnel from the Delhi Police and CRPF took positions at vantage points for armed retaliation. A fierce shoot-out ensued.

One terrorist, later identified as Mohammad, ran towards gate one, firing his AK-56 rifle indiscriminately at the security personnel. As he neared the gate, a bullet, fired by a CRPF jawan on duty, hit him. At the same time, a hand grenade he was carrying exploded, possibly hit by another bullet, and the terrorist collapsed near gate one—the gate used by all MPs except the prime minister, the Speaker of the Lok Sabha and the vice president, who have other designated gates of entry.

When the remaining four terrorists at gate eleven realized that the security forces on their side of the wall had ample firepower, they decided to jump over it and run along the central edifice, a direction that was opposite to that taken by Mohammad. What they didn't anticipate was that there was adequate security there as well, which had by then taken strategic positions. The CRPF fired at the running terrorists, and three of them, later identified as Rana, Raja and Hamza, fell in a heap on the porch of gate nine. The last one, identified as Haider, kept running until he too was shot dead and fell on the porch of gate five—the gate used by the prime minister of India. Later, an AK-47 rifle with a grenade launcher was found next to his body.

The Ambassador car—with registration number DL 3C J 1527—that the terrorists had used was found near gate eleven, the site of the commencement of the attack. Later, investigation revealed that the car had been bought from a second-hand car dealer in Karol Bagh. Interestingly, the car had changed hands five times before Mohammad bought it.

The firing stopped after about fifty minutes. By then all five terrorists had been killed. Five Delhi policemen, one female constable of the CRPF, two Watch and Ward staffers and a gardener of the Central Public Works Department (CPWD) fell to the terrorists' bullets. In addition, sixteen security men, most of them from CRPF, were injured.

* * *

The incident shook the country. Atal Bihari Vajpayee, the prime minister of India, thundered, 'The punishment will be as big as the crime.' L.K. Advani, the Union home minister, described the incident as 'the most alarming act of terrorism in the history of the two decades of Pak-sponsored terrorism. We will liquidate the terrorists and their sponsors, whoever they are, and wherever they are.'

Shrichand Kriplani, a BJP leader from Rajasthan, declared, 'The government should do what America has done in Afghanistan and what Israel is doing in Palestine. The government should not shy away from attacking Pakistan.'

Robert Blackwill, the US ambassador to India, observed, 'It was no different in its objective from the terror attack of September 11.'

The US government announced, 'India should take appropriate action.'

The Congress party, the main opposition party, said it would support 'any well-considered step'.

Pakistan's General Pervez Musharraf condemned the attack but warned India 'against any precipitous action by its government. This would lead to serious repercussions.' Pakistan denied any hand in the incident and alleged that India may have stage-managed the incident for its own political purposes.

* * *

I do not know what the immediate aftermath of this event was in other government organizations, but the CBI was abuzz with the anticipation that the investigation of the case, in all likelihood, would come to it. Therefore, it was no surprise when I got a call from my immediate superior in the bureau who said, 'Neeraj, I hope you know what is happening at the Parliament House. Why don't you go visit the site?' I left immediately, excited that I had been chosen to investigate such an important case, several thoughts swirling in my mind. Whom should I choose to be a part of my team? Would we succeed in cracking the case? Of course, the Intelligence Bureau and the Special Cell of the Delhi Police would be there to help us, I thought to myself.

However, these questions were fated to go unanswered. As I neared the iron gate of Sansad Bhawan on the Vijay Chowk side, a call from my boss jolted me out of my reverie. He asked me to return to headquarters.

'Your presence at the scene of the crime may give the media the impression that the case has already been transferred to the CBI. It will cause unnecessary confusion. So, please come back.'

I had to beat a hasty retreat and returned to the CBI headquarters with disappointment and a heavy heart.

* * *

In the Delhi Police, and possibly in other government departments as well, December is normally vacation time for most public servants as schools break for winter holidays. In a common room of the Special Cell headquarters on Lodhi Road sat several officers of the cell, trying to figure out who should proceed on leave and when to ensure that the cell had at least a few officers on duty. Suddenly, they saw the images of the terror attack on the television, much like we in the CBI had.

The Special Cell guys knew that that was the end of their vacation plans and they were all in for a long haul. They picked up their helmets, bulletproof jackets and their AKs and rushed to the spot. They were led by ACP Rajbir Singh, who headed a fine team of crack detectives that included inspectors Mohan Chandra Sharma, Hriday Bhushan, Lalit Negi, Sanjay Dutt, Govind Sharma, Badrish Dutt and many others.

The crime scene was a picture of chaos and confusion. There was worry that there could be a sixth terrorist in hiding somewhere inside the parliament complex. A couple of stray shots had been heard after the gun battle had ceased, giving rise to this speculation. When a long silence followed, those fears abated, and the security forces began to comb every nook and cranny of the Parliament House, both inside and outside the building. An all-clear sign was given after considerable time and people slowly began to emerge from hiding.

The National Security Guard (NSG) bomb squad had been summoned and on arrival they systematically examined the bodies of the terrorists, starting with Mohammad's, which was lying near gate one. After removing hand grenades and improvised explosive devices (IEDs) from his backpack, they allowed the Special Cell boys to carry out the remaining part of the search. Then they moved to Haider's body, lying near gate five, and lastly, to the bodies of Raja, Rana and Hamza. Detectives from the cell followed suit, carrying out the body searches in the same order. The bodies were later identified by these names by other arrested co-accused, mainly Afzal Guru.

It had been quite some time since the last bullet had been fired. Yet the parliamentarians were still too scared to come out of the Parliament House. The Watch and Ward staff were doing their best to convince the parliamentarians that it was all over, and they could leave the premises safely. However, the parliamentarians demanded that security make a safe passage for them by standing in a line, hand-in-hand, on either side of the porch, effectively creating two human shields. It was only when their demand was met that our lawmakers emerged from the citadel of democracy, one after the other in single file, cowering and shivering in fear. They walked between the human walls, crouching with their hands over their heads, quickly got into their vehicles and left. A few of them crouched down on the floors of their cars.

There is another amusing story, apocryphal though, that when the door-to-door search of the Parliament was under way, a certain cabinet minister was found hiding under his office table by a Delhi Police officer. Soon after the officer stepped into the room, the minister's mobile phone rang, giving his hiding place away. The officer's immediate reaction was to cock his pistol and challenge the man to come out with his hands on his head. To his horror, the officer saw the cabinet minister emerge from under the table.

The Special Cell carried out a proper search of the crime scene. The bodies of the five slain terrorists were searched, one by one. The militants had come heavily armed with automatic assault rifles, pistols, hand and rifle grenades, electronic detonators, spare ammunition, explosives in the form of IEDs such as tiffin bombs, and a sophisticated bomb kept in the boot of the car. Commenting on the weaponry and explosives much later, the Delhi High Court, while hearing the appeal of the convicted accused, observed: 'The fire power was awesome, enough to engage a battalion, and had the attack succeeded, the entire building with all inside would have perished.'

Besides the weapons, ammunition, hand grenades and grenade launchers found on them, small pieces of paper with five Indian mobile numbers and two Dubai numbers were recovered from each one of the dead jihadis. They carried fake identity cards of 'Xansa Webcity', which bore a common contact number, 98xxx89429. A fake ID of Cybertech Computer Hardware Solutions in the name of Ashiq Hussain was found on the dead body of Mohammad.

Arms, ammunition, binoculars, batteries and daggers were recovered from the car used by the attackers. Ownership documents of the car and a map of Delhi were also found.

In its boot lay an IED, made of 30 kilograms of explosive material, which was removed by the bomb disposal squad of the NSG. Had the car bomb exploded at any time, it would have caused devastating damage.

The bodies of the terrorists were shifted to Lady Hardinge Medical College Hospital for post-mortem and identification.

The telephone numbers that were found written on the slips of paper recovered from the terrorists' bodies were 98xxx10816, 98xxx11085, 98xxx44860, 98xxx02438 and 98xxx59315. The two Dubai-based telephone numbers that were also found in the pockets of the slain men were 0097150xxx6899 and 0097150xxx83340. Their analysis led to the finding that the terrorists had been in touch with the numbers 98xxx89429 (later found to be of one Mohammad Afzal); 98xxx73506 (later found to be that of Shaukat Hussain Guru) and 98xxx81228 (later found to be that of S.A.R. Geelani). It was also established that Geelani's number had been receiving calls from a satellite phone that was later found to belong to Ghazi Baba—the area commander of Jaish-e-Mohammed (JeM; a Pakistani jihadi group fighting for the 'liberation' of Kashmir) in India.

On 14 December 2001, the day after the attack, an incoming call from Srinagar to the mobile number 98xxx81228, registered in the name of S.A.R. Geelani, was intercepted. The conversation was in Kashmiri, which was immediately translated into Hindi by our officers. Geelani was heard speaking excitedly in support of the attack. On the same day, another incoming call from Srinagar, on mobile number 98xxx73506, was intercepted. In this call, a lady, later identified as Afsan Guru aka Navjot Sandhu, was heard speaking to Shaukat Hussain Guru, inquiring about his well-being and that of Afzal Guru.

Surveillance was mounted at the residence of Geelani in Mukherjee Nagar, and on 15 December, sleuths of the Special Cell apprehended Sayyed Abdul Rehman Geelani. On interrogation, he confessed that he had knowledge of the attack on the Parliament and that 98xxx89249 was the number of Afzal Guru of Baramulla district in Jammu and Kashmir. Geelani further disclosed that Shaukat Hussain Guru, then residing in Mukherjee Nagar, was the user of the mobile number 98xxx73506.

Geelani was from the Baramulla district, as per his disclosure to the police. After completing his schooling in Baramulla Government School, he moved to Kakroli in the Muzaffarnagar district of Uttar Pradesh, where he studied the Quran and Arabic at a madrasa. Subsequently, he completed his BA degree from Lucknow and his MA degree from Zakir Hussain College in Delhi University. In 1995, after completing an MPhil in Arabic, he began to pursue his PhD in Arabic from Delhi University and also to teach at Rajdhani College, Delhi.

During the time he was pursuing his postgraduate degree, Geelani met a Kashmiri youngster, Shaukat Hussain Guru, in Delhi. Shaukat also belonged to Baramulla. As both of them were from the same district, they began to meet often and became good friends. Shaukat shared with him the details of his love affair with a Sikh girl, Navjot Sandhu. Geelani married the two of them in a small ceremony in which he officiated as the maulvi. Navjot Sandhu was converted to Islam by Geelani and given the name Afsan Guru.

Geelani met Shaukat and Afsan Guru often and during one such meeting, Shaukat introduced him to his first cousin Afzal Guru, who also belonged to Baramulla. Whenever Afzal was in town, they would meet and discuss the 'ongoing jihadi freedom struggle' to liberate Kashmir.

During his interrogation, besides the above-mentioned facts, Geelani disclosed that nearly two months before the Parliament House attack, during one of his meetings with Afzal, he was introduced to one Mohammad, who had come from Pakistan and belonged to JeM. Shaukat, Afzal, Mohammad and Geelani shared details of a plan to carry out a fedayeen attack on the Parliament House in New Delhi. Geelani was also told that four other members of JeM had come to Delhi with arms, ammunition and explosives. Money for the operation was arranged by hawala from Dubai.

Geelani also disclosed that he, along with Afzal and Shaukat, had been in touch with the five JeM terrorists from Pakistan who stormed into the parliament complex on 13 December 2001. Afzal was the main coordinator for the said mission. He further stated that meetings were held in Shaukat's house in Mukherjee Nagar, during which Shaukat and Afzal, along with the other five terrorists, had discussed the plan to carry out the attack on the Indian parliament.

After Geelani's interrogation, the investigation team raided a first-floor flat in Mukherjee Nagar and arrested Afsan Guru aka Navjot Sandhu, wife of Shaukat Hussain. The mobile phone with the number 98xxx73506 was recovered from her possession. Some calls that had been made from this mobile were to the phone of her husband Shaukat, who had left for Srinagar with Afzal soon after the terror attack. Afsan Guru admitted that she had been aware of the plan to attack the Indian Parliament as several conspiratorial meetings had been held in her presence at her house in Mukherjee Nagar.

The information about Shaukat's and Afzal's escape to Srinagar was shared by the investigating team with the Srinagar Police, who apprehended the duo at a truck stand in Srinagar. A laptop along with accessories, one mobile phone and Rs 10 lakh were recovered from them. A team from the Special Cell rushed to Srinagar and took custody of the two accused nabbed by the Srinagar Police, seized the recovered articles and brought them back the same day. The said truck was brought back to Delhi later by another team of the Special Cell.

Afzal was a storehouse of information. He had become a militant after completing his schooling from Government School, Sopore, in Baramulla. In 1990, he joined the Jammu Kashmir Liberation Front (JKLF) and crossed over to Pakistan. He underwent extensive training for over two months at a JeM training camp located at Muzaffarabad in Pakistan-occupied Kashmir (PoK). The camp was run under the aegis of the ISI—Pakistan's rogue intelligence agency—which was determined to cause terror and spread chaos in India.

After completing his training in Muzaffarabad, Afzal was infiltrated into India by his handlers in March 1990. He started a small business, supplying surgical instruments in Srinagar, and visited Delhi often in connection with his work. Whenever he came to Delhi he would stay at Mukherjee Nagar with his cousin Shaukat, who encouraged him to study further through a Delhi University correspondence course.

Afzal graduated in 1994 but continued with his business, which kept him shuttling between Delhi and Srinagar.

In February 2001, he met one Tariq Ahmed at a chemist's shop in Lal Chowk, Srinagar. Tariq struck up a friendship with Afzal and gradually motivated him to join the fight to 'liberate' Kashmir. Tariq confessed to Afzal that he himself belonged to JeM. He exhorted Afzal to join JeM and become a part of an important mission that the outfit had launched.

Tariq introduced Afzal to one Mohammad at Batmalu Masjid in Srinagar. Afzal was told that Mohammad was a Pakistani national, deputed to carry out a fedayeen attack in Delhi, for which Afzal should create a base in Delhi. During his next visit to Delhi, Afzal motivated his cousin Shaukat to become a part of the conspiracy. He also asked Shaukat to find him a safe hideout for a group of terrorists, who were to come to Delhi soon for the mission. Shaukat arranged a room in a boys' hostel in Christian Colony, Mukherjee Nagar.

During his next visit to Srinagar, Tariq took Afzal to meet Ghazi Baba aka Doctor—a Pakistani national and the supreme commander of JeM in India. Ghazi Baba, who operated out of Adu hills in Pahalgam in Jammu and Kashmir, disclosed to Afzal that a fedayeen attack in Delhi was being planned and encouraged the latter to take care of Mohammad, who was the leader of the chosen team, and provide him logistical support in Delhi.

After a few days, Afzal brought Mohammad to Delhi. Mohammad brought a laptop and lots of money with him. He was put up at the boys' hostel in Mukherjee Nagar. Subsequently, on one of his many trips to Srinagar, Afzal met and then escorted four other JeM terrorists, namely, Raja, Rana, Hamza and Haider, to Delhi. They were put up in Gandhi Vihar in north-west Delhi. These four terrorists brought with them four AK rifles, twelve loaded magazines, three pistols with ammunition, fifteen grenade shells, detonators, two remote-control devices and wireless transceivers hidden in their luggage.

Ten days before the attack on the Parliament House, Afzal, Afsan Guru and Shaukat met with the five JeM fedayeens— Mohammad, Haider, Rana, Raja and Hamza—at Shaukat's house. During this meeting, it was decided to carry out a reconnaissance of the Parliament House in advance, for which they would need a motorcycle. Afzal and Mohammad bought a second-hand Yamaha motorcycle (registration number HR 51 E 5768) from a shop in Naiwalan in Karol Bagh, Delhi. Using this motorcycle, Mohammad and Afzal recced the route between their safe house and Sansad Bhawan.

Mohammad, accompanied by Afzal, then bought a white Ambassador from Karol Bagh with the registration number DL 3C J 1527. He had a red VIP beacon fitted on it so that it could pass as a government car. A car park label for Parliament House, downloaded from the Internet, was affixed to the front windscreen, much like it is done in other MPs' cars.

Thirty kilograms of ammonium nitrate and 4 kilograms each of sulphur and aluminium powder were purchased from Tilak Bazar in north Delhi to make IEDs. A steel container that could hold 30 kilograms of explosive material, and five containers for making tiffin bombs were purchased from Khari Baoli.

Five mobile phones, six SIM cards, five pairs of cargo trousers, five camouflage T-shirts, five jackets and five pairs of commando shoes from the Tibetan market at Majnu-ka-Tilla in north Delhi; three police uniforms from Kingsway Camp; and five backpacks from Chandni Chowk were purchased so that the fedayeens could dress as commandos during the forthcoming action.

The terrorists also prepared for themselves fake IDs of Xansa Webcity, a computer education school located at 37, Bungalow Road, Kamla Nagar. These cards were forged versions of the original identity card of the training institute under fake names such as Rohail Sharma, Raju Lal, Sanjay Kaul and so on.

Having made all these preparations, on the morning of 13 December 2001, Afzal and Shaukat met Mohammad and his four associates at their new safe house in Gandhi Vihar in north-west Delhi. Mohammad handed over a laptop and Rs 10 lakh to Afzal and asked him to give the laptop to Tariq at Lal Chowk in Srinagar on 16 December. Further, Mohammad asked Afzal to accompany Tariq when he went to meet Ghazi Baba and in turn hand over the laptop to the JeM commander.

Mohammad also instructed Afzal to turn on the TV on 13 December—the day of the attack—at 11.30 a.m. and let Mohammad know the names of the VIP MPs who were present in the Parliament House. However, when Mohammad called Afzal at 11.25 a.m., Afzal informed him that he was nowhere near a TV set. Afzal called Shaukat to ask him to switch on his TV and let him know who was present inside the Parliament House. By the time Shaukat could do so, Mohammad and his four associates were already inside the parliament complex and were in the midst of their operation.

On 10 December—three days before the incident—Mohammad, during a conversation with Afzal, had shared details of his involvement in the hijacking of Indian Airlines flight 814 (IC 814) in December 1999, when the said flight was forcibly taken to Kandahar in Afghanistan. During the hijacking, Mohammad was addressed by the fake name 'Burger'. It was as a consequence of this hijacking that the Government of India had handed over the JeM supremo Maulana Masood Azhar along with Omar Sheikh and Mushtaq Ahmed Zargar to the hijackers in exchange for the passengers of IC 814 held hostage. (Please see 'Story of Their Assassins'.)

Afzal's interrogation further revealed that the real objective of the terror attack was for the terrorists to get into the Parliament House, take some important MPs and ministers hostage, kill some others, and negotiate with the Government of India to secure Kashmir's liberation in exchange for the lives of the Indian politicians. It was no surprise, therefore, that the terrorists had come prepared for a long haul. They carried sufficient quantities of dry fruits and plastic rope, which were found during the body searches of the five slain terrorists. Carrying dry fruits for sustenance is a common practice amongst fedayeens who are sent on missions that may take days to complete. Dry fruits were also found on every terrorist brought down by security forces in the Mumbai attacks on 26 November 2008.

The plastic ropes found with the terrorists were meant to bind the hands and feet of hostages inside the Parliament House.

However, the terrorists' plan failed due to the bravery
of the security men, who successfully thwarted their
attempt.

* * *

After the attack, relations between India and Pakistan soured
to an extent that large-scale mobilization of the armies of both
nations took place along the Line of Control. The two nations
were on the brink of war when diplomatic intervention
from other countries prevented a flashpoint. Another
theory put forward by Adrian Levy and Cathy Scott-Clark—
authors of *The Siege*, which is based on the 26 November
attack on Mumbai, and *Exile*, which is on the last days of
Osama bin Laden—suggests that the motive behind the
Parliament House attack was to create tension between India
and Pakistan so that Pakistani army deployment along the
Afghan border was reduced. This would then allow Osama
bin Laden to escape into Pakistan as the battle of Tora Bora
between the US troops and Al-Qaeda raged in the aftermath
of the 11 September attacks.

On 14 May 2002, Afzal Guru, Shaukat Hussain Guru,
Sayyed Abdul Rehman Geelani, Afsan Guru aka Navjot
Sandhu along with Maulana Masood Azhar, Ghazi Baba aka
Doctor and Tariq Ahmed—three proclaimed offenders—had
charge sheets filed against them. Charges were framed under
various sections of the Indian Penal Code, the Prevention of
Terrorism Act 2002 (POTA) and the Explosive Substances
Act before the designated sessions court presided over by
Justice S.N. Dhingra.

Eighty witnesses were examined for the prosecution and ten witnesses on behalf of the accused, S.A.R Geelani. The trial concluded within six months and Afzal Guru, Shaukat Hussain Guru and S.A.R. Geelani were convicted.* Accused number four, namely, Navjot Sandhu aka Afsan Guru, was acquitted of all charges except Section 123 of the Indian Penal Code (concealing with intent to facilitate design to wage war against the Government of India), for which she was convicted and sentenced to imprisonment for five years.

The death sentence was imposed on the other three accused, namely, Afzal Guru, Shaukat Hussain Guru and S.A.R. Geelani. It was a huge victory for us in the Special Cell.

The appeal against the conviction of the accused was heard in the Delhi High Court. It was around this time that I had returned to the Delhi Police, after nine years of deputation in the CBI, and was working in the Special Cell. It was very important to have the best legal team possible to represent us when the Delhi High Court heard the appeals of the accused against the orders of the court. Our first choice was Gopal Subramanium, an eminent advocate known for his professional excellence and his incisive legal mind. However, it is never easy for the police to get a special counsel of their choice appointed in government cases. The common refrain

---

*   Afzal Guru, Shaukat Hussain Guru and S.A.R. Geelani were convicted for the offences under Sections 121, 121A, 122, Section 120B, read with Sections 302 and 307, read with Section 120B of IPC, subsections (2), (3) and (5) of Section 3 and Section 4(b) of POTA, and Sections 3 and 4 of Explosive Substances Act. The accused 1 and 2 were also convicted under Section 3(4) of POTA.

from the bureaucracy is to make do with the existing law officers of the government. It was with considerable difficulty that we acquired the necessary approval for Subramanium to represent us alongside the government counsel.

The Delhi High Court acquitted S.A.R. Geelani and Afzal Guru but upheld Shaukat Hussain Guru's and Afzal Guru's death sentences. Geelani, who according to the prosecution had played a vital role in the conspiracy that led to the attack on the Indian parliament, had received extensive support from his outraged colleagues and friends in Delhi University, who were certain that he was innocent. He was represented by the lawyer Nandita Haksar, and at the end of the High Court hearings, was acquitted.

In the Supreme Court, where Gopal Subramanium represented us with his team, the death sentence of Afzal was upheld but Shaukat was held guilty under Section 123 of the Indian Penal Code and sentenced to ten years of imprisonment. S.A.R. Geelani and Afzal Guru (accused no. 4) were acquitted by the Supreme Court.

Shaukat walked free nine months before his official date of release on account of his good behaviour in jail.

Eleven years, one month and twenty-seven days after the attack on the Indian parliament, Afzal Guru was hanged at 8 a.m. on 9 February 2013 in Tihar Jail, New Delhi. He had been on death row since 2002. He was buried in the prison itself after observing proper religious rites.

Afzal had no doubt engineered the 13 December 2001 attack on the Parliament House. He had worked out every minute detail for the fedayeens—their stay, fake identification documents, logistical support, mentorship, buying of explosives, the car to be used and the sneaking in of arms from outside Delhi. He had helped the militants reconnoitre the Parliament House several times to determine from which side they would gatecrash into its hallowed premises. And yet, the key conspirator had himself stayed away from the attack, perhaps because he had not had any prior training to undertake an attack of that scale and magnitude.

Afzal's hanging was mired in controversy. Omar Abdullah, the then chief minister of Jammu and Kashmir, described the execution as 'selective' and said that generations of Kashmiris would identify with him. He said that by not allowing Afzal to meet with his family before he was executed, the Indian government had set an unwarranted precedent. Kashmir was under curfew the day Afzal was hanged, and as the news broke, there was much unrest in several parts of the country, including Delhi.

On 30 August 2003, Shah Nawaz Khan aka Ghazi Baba, the JeM mastermind behind the attack, was killed in an encounter with the Border Security Force in Noorbagh, Srinagar.

Maulana Masood Azhar, the Pakistan-based founder and leader of JeM, could not be arrested and was therefore declared a proclaimed offender on 1 April 2002. Readers may recall that he had been released from custody in December 1999 by the Government of India in exchange for the passengers of the hijacked flight IC 814. However, in a major diplomatic victory, India later succeeded in getting him declared a global terrorist by the United Nations Security Council.

The identity of Tariq Ahmed, the elusive JeM operative who had played a critical role in the operation from Kashmir, was never fully established. All that was known was that he was a Pakistani. He was never arrested, and he too was declared a proclaimed offender in the case on 1 April 2002.

* * *

When the 9/11 attacks took place in the US, several conspiracy theories were put forward, one more preposterous than the other. One such theory claimed that the collapse of the World Trade Center was the result of controlled demolitions rather than the impact of the jets flown into them by the fedayeens of Al-Qaeda. Another theory was that the US government had advance intelligence about the attacks but deliberately chose to ignore it so that they could attack Afghanistan. There are a few others, but none of note.

In our country too, sceptics abound. I recall when I succeeded in getting members of Tiger Memon's family to return to India from Dubai, several naysayers talked of a 'deal' between the CBI and the Memons. Their contention was that the Memons had returned to India of their own accord because they had been assured that the CBI would go easy on them and they would be acquitted. But the Memons were tried like any other accused, three of them were sentenced to life imprisonment and Yaqub Memon was hanged. The conspiracy theorists' loud voices went silent on the occurrence of these events. Similarly, in 2013 when the Delhi Police unravelled the Indian Premier League spot-fixing scandal, a senior journalist interviewed me for a prestigious TV channel. I was then the commissioner of police, Delhi. The journalist alleged that the entire operation had been stage-managed by us to improve our image, which had deteriorated following the ghastly Nirbhaya incident. I replied to the journalist on camera, rather sarcastically, that I was mighty pleased with the resourcefulness of my force, which could make over thirty people, including three prominent cricketers, agree to get arrested and go to jail to assist us in bolstering our public image.

It was not surprising, therefore, to hear similar stories about the attack on the Parliament House. In a whisper campaign, the then ruling party—BJP—was accused of staging the terror attack to distract public attention from the Bangaru Laxman fiasco, where the BJP party chief was caught on camera accepting money to assist phony arms dealers bag government contracts (see 'Story of Their Assassins'). Sundry cynics, most of them 'well educated', subscribe to this view till date. But, more shockingly, many naysayers felt that the security forces deployed at the parliament complex need not have given their lives to fight the terrorists. The cynics, some from within the government, would have been happier if the terrorists had been given a safe passage into the Parliament House so that they could do away with as many parliamentarians as possible. Little do they realize the repercussions that would have followed, and what the aftermath of such an event would have been. Our country would have certainly gone to war with Pakistan and faced other catastrophic eventualities.

Be that as it may, the terror attack on the Parliament House was easily one of the dastardliest acts of Pakistan-based terrorists. Providence had willed their plan to fail. The little wall near gate eleven proved to be the terrorists' nemesis. The response of the security forces was commendable, leading to the gunning down of the attackers. The closing of the gates of the parliament by the Watch and Ward staff was another masterly stroke. That five Delhi Police personnel, a CRPF constable, two Watch and Ward staffers and a gardener lost their precious lives was the price we had to pay to protect the citadel of our democracy and our elected parliamentarians. We, as Indians, should never forget their sacrifice.

Acknowledgements

Thanks to the persuasive skills of S. Hussain Zaidi, the celebrated crime writer of Mumbai, and the confidence shown by Milee Ashwarya of Penguin Random House in me, *Khaki Files* is a reality today. My indolence and procrastination made me cross many a deadline agreed upon during the writing of the book. Milee and Gurveen Chadha showed remarkable patience and magnanimity with me and gave me a rope longer than I deserved. I owe them a special gratitude for bearing with me and letting me take my time. I am also grateful to the editorial team headed by Milee, for making a book out of the rather haphazard scribblings of my recollections.

Sayantan Chakravarty, editor and publisher of *India Empire* magazine, is arguably one of the finest investigative journalists this country has seen. Earlier, he had covered quite a few events described in the book as a senior correspondent for another leading magazine. I couldn't have found a better storehouse of information than him. He held my hand, much as he had done when I wrote *Dial D for Don*, for which I can never thank him enough.

My children Arunima, Ankita, Manav and Kushagra were my first sounding boards. Ankita and Manav came forward to take dictations from me over long sessions. I know I don't need to thank any of them but they are deserving of my blessings.

Much like my first book, this one too could not have been possible without the support of my colleagues, who were not only by my side when the investigations I have described in the book took place but also helped me with facts and figures, as I had no notes or records to bank on. S.M. Bhaskar was my ACP when I investigated the lottery frauds of Delhi in 1992. Pramod Kushwaha, an ACP in the Special Cell, played the leading role in the cyber investigation that prevented what could have been a catastrophic terror attack on Delhi. S.C. Jha, O.P. Chhatwal and Raman Tyagi were part of my team that investigated and prosecuted the perpetrators of the serial train blasts of December 1993. My batchmate Shailendra Sagar and Dheeraj Mathur, my staff officer when I was DG, Delhi Prisons, provided invaluable inputs for the story on a jail inmate. Ishwar Singh, now ACP, was a young sub-inspector when the investigation against serial killers from an erstwhile criminal tribe was conducted under my charge. Hriday Bhushan and Lalit Negi, both inspectors in the Special Cell of the Delhi Police, helped me with the chapter on the conspiracy to kill two famous Delhi journalists. Chhaya Sharma, ACP Rajender Singh, inspectors Rituraj and Gagan Bhaskar, sub-inspector Arvind Kumar filled in the missing gaps in the Nirbhaya story. I am beholden to all of them for providing me with the finer details that make the stories in this book authentic and accurate.

A special thanks to my senior colleague Raja Vijay Karan for writing the foreword to my second book too, again at a very short notice. His abiding love and kindness for my family and me have always overwhelmed me.

For their encouraging words, I am grateful to: Milee Ashwarya, the dynamic editor-in-chief of Penguin Random House; Gurveen Chadha, my young editor; Shreya Dhawan and Joseph Antony, my line editors; and Neeraj Nath, who designed the cover. I owe a special debt of gratitude to them for bringing the manuscript to this present form.

I owe a special word of gratitude to my old friend Rajdeep Sardesai, who, despite his overwhelming preoccupations, wrote an endorsement for the book at a very short notice. I deeply value his words of appreciation and shall never forget his kind gesture.

Neeraj Pandey is a film personality with a difference. Besides his prodigious talent in directing and writing films, he scores over his peers in human qualities. I gave him very little time for writing a few words about the book. Despite his more-than-busy schedule, he found time to send his endorsement. I thank him from the bottom of my heart.

Lastly, the real motivating force that kept me going was the appreciation I had received from readers of *Dial D for Don*. On social media not only had they kept in touch with me but also insisted I write again. I thank them for their belief in me. I sincerely hope they like *Khaki Files* as well.